DARREN KEITH RUSSELL

NOTORIOUS
INSIDE THE SPIDER

TRUE CRIME

Notorious Inside The Spider
Copyright © 2025 by Darren Keith Russell

All rights reserved. Th is book or any portion thereof may not be reproduced or used in any manner whatsoever without the express written permission of the publisher except for the use of brief quotation in a book review.

ISBN: 979-8-89175-184-2 (sc)
ISBN: 979-8-89175-185-9 (ebk)

CHAPTER 1

Roger The Dodger

My older brothers marijuana plants were growing well. He grew them with the next door neighbour as they were both 15 and best mates. They showed me in exchange for 2 cigarettes. My mother gave me $2 every day for school lunch and with 90c I would buy cigarettes. For 3 cigarettes I swapped David Hall for his lunch and morning tea. His mum made the best lunches. They were always packed in foil or paper with a cake and a frozen Drink. The drink would keep them cold inside the lunchbox it was great. My brother and his mate were hopeless with money and always asking me for cigarettes. One time I even paid his drug debt. Linden was my brothers mate David's little brother. "I know where's there's heaps of them" Linden said after they showed us the plants. Linden was 11 and still went to primary school. "fuck off Linden you lying little cunt" David said but Linden insisted and was then punched for lying. 5 months had past, David and Wayne drove my grandmother's Volkswagen to pick me up from school. "Go over and grab Linden" my brother ordered, so I did. "your getting flogged if those plants aren't there" they told Linden. Linden gave directions swearing it was true. He used to stay at his friends after soccer and found them while playing in the bush. Just like he said there were hundreds of them. Approximately 2 acres of 5 to 6 feet tall plants.

There was a creek bed below a small cliff face that seemed to overflow when it rained. The run off water from the cliff face overflowed the creek and made a silt plain for acres beside it. It wouldn't have needed watering, it was a perfect spot. The brothers handed us garbage bags and we started stuffing them full. There was a couple of bundles of plants wrapped in wire hanging from the trees and we found a vegemite jar that had some compressed head and white powder in it. The white powder would have most likely been heroin or speed which we new nothing about in those days so it got thrown away. The bud was taken by the brothers. I told Linden to only pull off the leaves and any parts of head. That way we could fit more into the bags. The brothers wouldnt listen "it takes too much time" they said stuffing entire plants into there bags. When it dried Linden and I had four times more weed. Wayne and David's was mainly branches from not removing the stems. As a result they took mine and Lindens as we had only filled 4 garbage bags between us. Angry I went and saw my best friend Darmo as his older brother had a license. We borrowed his mums car and took as much as we could but there was heaps left. It wasn't enough so I rounded up 2 cars and went back for more. 3 guys with balaclavas came running out the bush as we climbed through the fence. Scared we ran to the cars. As we drove away the guys pulled motorcycles up from the long grass. We thought we were in danger but it was John Tamer and his older brother Dale with a guy called Snelly just behind them. "There's fucking heaps" they screamed signalling us to go over. "we'll be back for more" they said then rode off. 4 years later I was at a older friends house. His name was Trevor and he was 32. I was there with a 16 year old friend called Thommo when Dean Poman turned up. "I need a lift to get some weed" he said. He asked if I would take him to trim his fathers plants as I didn't smoke weed and he trusted I wouldn't steal them. Keeping my motorcycle out of sight was easy. There was a huge concrete pipe under the road so we parked in it. We cut across other peoples property so he followed fence lines to work out where he was. "wait here" he said. "they are just ahead of us". He told me he'd be back but as soon as he walked off I followed. After they dried and smoked the weed Dean Poman left. Trevor The older one asked if I had seen them. "Did you see the plants" he said. He told me Deans father grew crops every year for crooked police. Dean had been shooting his mouth off a fair bit and apparently $50,000 the father had been paid in advance. It was a hydroponic crop probably one of the first and definitely the first I've ever seen. There were 56 plants in total grown in perlite. The root systems only grew 2 inches deep but were very matted together. They were grown in pots with plugs in the bottom with drainer trays. You pour on a nutrient watering solution and the perlite soaks it up like a sponge. Once the perlite absorbs the solution you pull the plugs and drain off the excess. I thought of being caught for stealing them and realized I could be killed. They would know it was me so I told Thommo we were only taking half. That way when they were going to kill me I could say "at least I left you half". I would point out it's the fathers fault for showing off to the son. Not long after we transplanted them the mother came to look through Thommos car. It had white perlite balls through it everywhere but we cleaned it thoroughly. We stuck to our story and said "don't know what your talking about" but she knew it was us. She was receiving half the money for alimony and wasn't happy. They kept a close eye on us for a long time. They waited for us to slip assuming we would be seen with weed. Most would have sold some but we transplanted and kept it growing instead. Detective Blanchette from blue murder the movie was busted shortly after. Blanchette was tied in with Roger Rogerson and lived on a property 2 streets away. Roger the dodger they called him. He was the most dangerous police officer in our history. They were his plants, It took me years to piece it together. Both crops were on the same property just at different ends. There was a runway for light aircraft and Deans dad was a pilot. It was a particular strain of marijuana only found in Thailand. It occasionally produced a throw back to a one fingered leaf plant. During the winter after the first time, I went back to have a look. I found three very unusual plants. It was hard to get marijuana to grow in Sydney during winter. One plant was two straight stems with no leaves just bud and the buds were on the tips in clusters the size of cobs of corn. Another was just a cluster of buds shaped like a Christmas tree. The third was unlike anything I've ever seen. It had all branches, no buds and only one fingered leaves. I figured they'd been flying drugs from Thailand. Heroin comes from Thailand and that's also what Roger Rogerson was known to be involved in. Roger is now serving a life sentence for murder after killing a drug dealer with another x detective.

CHAPTER 2

Australia's Most Notorious Serial Killer: Ivan Milat

I grew up in the same area as Ivan and worked at a coal mine his brother worked at. Ivan also drank at Bargo hotel, that's how he got the name Bargo Bill. Bill its what the publican called him. My brother lived at Bargo and sometimes I would hitch hike over to visit. I used to walk into the pub and ask the publican "hey would anyone be going down the highway past the Campbelltown exit" and he would say "Bill will be going that way in about half a schooner if you can wait that long" Ivan's seat belt was rigged to trap you into the car. He was cunning and would do things like hand you a opened can of coke and say "here I just opened it you look thirsty" It would be laced with drugs. When you went to clamp the seatbelt in the button would fall out. The seatbelt fastener was a different design to what it is now and in those days the button you pressed to unlock your seatbelt pressed inwards not downwards. The button you press to unfasten your seatbelt holds a spring loaded pin that clicks and locks thru the square shaped hole in your seatbelt. Ivan's button and pin would fall out leaving a hole straight through the female part of the fastener and he would say "silly thing does that all the time I'll get it fixed one day" and he'd laugh. then he would find a zippy tie and say he would cut it off with his knife when you needed to get out. Most people don't and can't say no and they are trapped into the car seat.

I used to hitchhike Goulburn to Campbelltown since I was 15 years old. I hitchhiked with my older brother who would visit his girlfriend in Batemans Bay. One time he forced me to return home on my own. It was a spring morning. My brother and his girlfriend dropped me at the turnoff to hitchhike from Batemans bay to Braidwood. I got a lift pretty fast with a young guy and his girlfriend as they were concerned to see such a young boy on his own. They drove me all the way to Braidwood and bought me a hamburger and coke as I had no money. From there I had to get from Braidwood to Goulbourn before hitchhiking from Goulburn to Campbelltown. It was about 600klm trip and would take all day. Again I was lucky as A mini bus with religious people from a religious sect stopped to pick me up. We always heard rumours about religious cults near Goulburn and now I new it was true. It was a long ride and they tried and tried to coax me into going with them and joining there sect. After a couple of hours I arrived in Goulbourn. Ivan used to wait at the end of the bridge coming out of Goulburn. He would drink at the pub and could watch when a hitchhiker would walk and stand at the start of the princess highway where the cars could pull over. It was the only way out of Goulbourn and the only place you could stand and hitchhike. Ivan would see a person standing there and get into his car and pick them up. As soon I had got there to the spot where you had to stand and put my thumb out Ivan was there. "Jump in kid" he said "and don't forget to fasten your seatbelt". When I went to plug the seat belt in the button fell out. "oh that does that all the time" he said before he rummaged through his console to pull out a zippy tie. "here use this" he said. "no its ok ill just hold it" I replied as I could sense straight away something wasn't right. "Good instincts" he joked. We were now doing at least 100 kilometres per hour along the freeway and he asked if I was scared? "For all you know I could be a serial killer" he said and again he laughed. Then he asked me again if I was scared so I replied "being scared never saved anyone" "for all you know I could be a killer to" I said. Ivan laughed and laughed and told me he liked me. He continued to joke saying I might just make it home. He managed to stay on the killer topic by asking if I was a killer what sort of killer would I be. Eventually I confessed that I wasn't a killer but did have rape fantasy's since I was 12 years old. We talked about that and that seemed to make him happy. Before I knew it he put his blinker on as we were approaching a side street. "I've just gotta pick something up" he said telling me I could wait on the corner until he got back or stay in the car. He pointed out the house and it was just off the highway so I chose to stay in the car. When he pulled up to the house he told me not to look in the glovebox. He said if I looked in the glovebox he would know and get very angry. As soon as he walked inside I looked in the glovebox. In the glovebox was a opened yellow envelope with a handgun sitting inside it. He wasn't long and came back to the car empty handed. After checking that I didn't look in the glovebox he went back to the house and brought out a long triangular case. He slid the case behind the front seats and started the car. "you looked in the glovebox didn't you" he said. I tried to say no but I have trouble lieing. I should have ran as soon as I saw the gun but I thought then he would know I looked in the glovebox. He got pretty angry pretty fast and took off speeding down the highway. It wasn't long before he made a hard left turn onto a road I was familiar with. It was a road that cut across to the area I lived in through a town called Douglas park. The road went up to the left then swung around parallel to the highway but sloped down to a one-way bridge. "get out of the car" he yelled after pulling over just before the start of the one way bridge. He yelled again to start running as he was going for the rifle. "make sure of it" was his 3rd command saying I had 20 seconds before he shoots. I ran straight up the road as there was a guide railing blocking me from running into the creek bed then something told me to turn left 90 degrees and run for the highway. In order to run to the highway I had to run up hill for a few seconds through re generated forest. Re generated forest is saplings planted after the machines had ripped up the ground when building the highway. "crack crack thooot thooot thooot" was the sound of the gun going off and the bullets snapping through the leaves. It was one of the most frightening experiences of my life. I was running so fast my legs were almost coming out from under me and im lucky I didn't trip over. I scrambled down the other side of the hill as fast as I could out onto the highway. I just stood out on the road as the cars weren't stopping and I could see him coming. A person with a English accent pulled up in a white Van and I always believed it could have been Paul Onions. Maybe that's how he got the story for police about Ivan chasing us up the road. He always said someone else was there but never really explained his day leading up to the story he told. Ivan drove up beside the van waving the hand gun around. He terrorized us for a few kilometres and then sped off. When I got out at the Wilton over pass I went and rang my father reverse charge and he came and picked me up. He didn't believe me when I told him so I just left it at that. Occasionally I've told friends about it but always assumed it was a hard story to believe or for people to accept.

CHAPTER 3

Inside The Spider

It was the year 2021. Manitou had been quite restless. His attempts to gain my attention had become more and more frequent. He cant talk, he sends visuals and it takes some thought to reveal what he may mean but over the years its getting easier. Lately its gotten so bad I can no longer write my books and it seems he is desperately trying to get things through to me. As I type he alters the words trying to tell me things. Visions of mars have became more and more common. I'm sure there is giant spiders and the big white domes are spider eggs. He has proven this by alerting me to visions of NASA polluting space by burning rocket fuel. When rocket fuel burns it leaves behind a carbon residue no different to the soot that builds in a chimney and space is supposed to be a sterile environment. Each tiny particle contains single charged atoms and dozens of hydrogen molecules are attached. Hydrogen molecules contain microscopic life similar to the mites that crawl on peoples skin. The mites that crawl on people have mites that crawl on them and so on. In the vacuum of space there is no gravity allowing these microscopic beasts to evolve both rapidly and very large. We are in grave danger but for now I must go back in time to where Manitou and I first met for you to understand.

I was 15 years old when I had my first epileptic seizure but I don't remember much. This time however was very different. I had just joined the Australian Army and was combing my hair in front of the bathroom mirror. All of a sudden my arms and legs locked up as if a huge cramp had consumed every muscle in my body. The pain was intense and like nothing I had ever felt in my life. I wanted to and needed to scream out so bad but was un able to and to be honest I would rather burn alive then experience it again. There was no way to release the feeling no way at all. My arms buckled and were waving around by themselves as if someone else was controlling them. As I begged for mercy I heard a high pitch frequency in the distance. It was so far away but it was coming closer and closer and it was clear it was coming for me. I was so scared! The noise got closer and louder as it came then boom like a bomb hit me and I was hurled across the room which left a huge imprint into the wall. I was still alive I just wasn't anywhere on earth that's for sure. It almost seemed as if I was in a spiralling tunnel travelling upwards. When I looked behind me there was just a open end out to space. I had walked forever. It was a very lonely walk but then after thinking that and thinking how long I had been walking everything changed in a instant. There was now square walls, 1 door to the left appeared and 2 doors to the right. The door on the left hand side had flashing lights and hustlers trying to sell me something and coax me in. The doors to the right had nothing and from memory 1 was closed. The only one open was very dim lit like late afternoon and it was very eerie in there. I Plundered and was weak for a moment and the hustlers had coaxed me in. Anything I wanted they told me absolutely anything was mine. They said I could go back to earth as anything I pleased so a 500cc grand prix motorcycle champion was what I chose as I had ridden motorcycles all my life. My bike was presented by Winfield models and already on the starting grid and I was dressed ready to race. I totally blitzed the entire field of competitors. I could ride as fast as I wanted my knees and elbows scraping the ground without fear and I loved the speed. Soon after I had won the race the climate changed cold and the landscape turned into a baron wasteland like the moon and mars mixed together, it was strange. There wasn't much fun anymore and the further I travelled the more daunting and lonely it became. I rode and rode to no avail but as I thought of turning back a hitchhiker was standing there with his thumb in the air. Beware the lone traveller is a automatic instinct these days but not then so I pulled up to ask for directions. He seemed nice enough "not to far from here" he said "pardon" I questioned him but he changed the subject as he looked my bike over. "Wooowee wow what a bike" he said asking for a lift. As I went to tell him I had no spare helmet he replied "your not wearing one out here surely" and chuckled "no police out these parts". He got on the back ensuring me it wasn't far. Travelling way too fast and accelerating through every gear I travelled a few kilometres while the hitchhiker gave me a thumbs up signalling to keep going faster. All of sudden the road turned to ice and the walls closed in a tunnel around me. I could hear the familiar high pitched sound coming so I laid the bike over on the ice and slid in fear. I must of been going 300 kilometres per hour. As I finally started to slow down the grade in the road started sloping and the noise was getting louder and louder coming for me from the opposite direction. I clawed the ice as hard as I could to slow me down. The fear was intense and the sound was deafening. A giant demon breathing fire roared its ugly head towards me but I was just out of its reach and the hitch hiker had turned into the devil and tried to cling on. I kicked my legs as hard as I could and kicked free. Walking back seemed to take several years at least but I eventually got there. Running had become my hobby and my only past time and my brain would switch off. Again I had a similar experience as the one I had before and after just about giving up hope the doors re appeared. I was faced with the same 3 doors. A dead end one way and a cliff edge staring back at space. Desperate I sat alone and cried. I missed my family and my girlfriend so much it had been so long. I sat crying and cried for what seemed another eternity. It was hopeless and at times I thought of going back and surrendering myself to the devil. Then it came to me. I remembered my grandmothers teachings and bible story's she had told me. I had not been baptized or christened to any faith so it was all I knew. As I walk through the valley of the shadow of death ill fear no evil as the lord is my Shepard. A few deep breaths and I walked into the lonely doorway. The wind howled across a grass cow paddock in the late afternoon. The further I went the darker it got and the valley became clear. Its very true what the bible says as ghosts and goblins come from every direction But you cant see them until they are just upon you. The more you fear the more real they become and I was touched by a few so I repeated the bible phrases over and over. As I walked the ghosts passed straight through but I'm sure if you continued to fear them they would be real. Once again as soon as the fear emotion was gone and I realized how far I had walked in a instant it was light and the valley disappeared. After all that time I was there at a cliff edge and it looked like earth in the distance. Finally I thought! There was a giant craft sailing across from the other world. There were hundreds of people waiting but when the ship pulled up my name was not on the list and they wouldn't let me board. "ITS NOT YOUR TIME" he shouted cracking his whip at me "you best get back there boy" he said and blew his whistle. I was broken hearted as time on earth must have been thousands of year into the future to travel space like that. It must have travelled at the speed of light as it seemed to warp like a beam. My family would be long gone I thought so I ran as fast as I could through that valley but instantly I was back at the doors. Spider web was tangled around me and I was naked as my clothes had long disappeared. This time a tubular corridor was about 50 metres from the edge. I had never read a book not a single one just a few pieces of Rampa Lampa the doctor from Tibet. It was a book on astral travel and the power of belief. This time I didn't hesitate. Write or wrong I was jumping as I was sick of the place so I ran about 5 steps toward the cliff edge and in an a instant I was in the tube on the other side. A god like ora was awaiting me "ha ha ha ha ha" he laughed "enjoying yourself Darren Keith" "Still a long way to Tipperary isn't it? or is it? that all depends on you" he said. There was one door to a lonely picture theatre with a projector playing in front. What's playing I asked "whatever you want to see Darren "advanced mining techniques you've a keen eye ha ha ha"" he laughed. I saw many futuristic pieces of footage and footage from my life, past, present and some from the future and then finally I fell asleep. Tired I dreamt of heaven and my family but they were totally different people to the ones on earth. Heaven wasnt a planet it was a giant spaceship so large its uncomprehendible and I was on a smaller spaceship coming in to dock. Everyone looked exactly the same except my wife and family but they looked the same to everyone else only I could see there true identity and I couldn't see anyone else's family either. I think everyone looking the same was to remove jealousy from the place as you cant want what you cant see. My memory of earth was a distant un important memory as I was now flooded with century's of memory's I had been programmed to forget and when shown to my room there was everything inside. Anything you could think of wanting to do it appeared and even when I had sex with my wife her appearance would change to what pleased me the most. When I woke I kept hearing this clicking sound and for the life of me I couldn't work out where it was coming from. Then all of a sudden I caught something out of the corner of my eye, it was a long black leg. Something told me to look down at my chest and there were two long skinny legs draped either side. Fuck me I thought its a huge a spider and I was terrified. It started moving and I've never been so scared in my life. It slowly creeped around and starred its ugly head into my face. It must have been tightly clung to the back of my neck. Appearing it didn't want to hurt me it kept trying to stick its fingers up my nose and it was quite insistent. I was now thinking it was a baby and must have been hungry. I eventually let it feel around in my nose and then it eventually climbed down and walked towards the door pausing and peering back at me I sensed it wanted me to follow. It seemed I had a lot more running to do as the dead ended tube was now a roadway. The spider grew quickly and soon I was able to ride it. We walked the winding roadway at first but I eventually got him running and when we got to the end of the road it was near to earth but still quite a jump down to the ground. I felt I could communicate with the spider as he did most things I thought. When I needed him to move he moved and when I needed him to stop he stopped. I got him to connect his web and we sailed on down to earth. My house was there and before I knew it I was staring down at my body crumpled on the floor. My father was trying to slap some life into me while my mother screamed. I awoke in hospital 3 days later with Kate Leons stroking my head. The Army was quick to send a discharge and my body felt like It had been pounded by baseball bats all over. Doctors said I had had some sort of epileptic convulsion but all the tests were negative. So tired I had seen Kates beautiful face and fell straight back to sleep. All I remember is her saying "hey there". In the years that followed I formed ganglion lumps in both my wrists and eventually they travelled to the middle of my forehead. It looks like I've got a third eye. Ganglion lumps are rumoured to be tiny spiders that live under the skin. Soon after a lump like a nipple appeared to grow to the right of my belly button. It was there for about a year but my girlfriend got weird about it so I agreed to have it cut out. The doctor that had seen it only did surgery on Thursdays and made a appointment for me to come back as it was only a Monday. That night in the shower I glanced down at the lump and it had changed. A big yellow coloured balloon was protruding out the end and as I went to touch it puss ran down onto my leg without me putting a finger on it. The lump then slowly vanished without a scar and it happened in front of my eyes in a couple of minutes. It re appeared about a year later like a wart right at the end of my tail bone. It stayed settled for about 5 years then one day whilst at work a guy said "hey Demo something is running down your leg". I only wore shorts at work so I reached around and wiped it. It was thick dark red blood. Later that day I worked out it was coming from the lump which was now a hole as round as my finger. Un able to take time off work I dealt with the bleeding daily carrying a roll of toilet paper. It was almost like a woman's period but non stop daily for 3 months and it was sore. At night it felt good to squeeze it a little to relieve the pressure. It wouldn't just bleed blood it would get infected as well. A few months later I got time off work so I went to see a doctor. I was working in the coal mines in a remote part of Queensland so Mackay was where I went. By the time I got to the doctors it had partly closed over but was still clearly visible. The doctor said it was a sebaceous sist and he explained it may have roots entangled in my bowl. He eventually said if I could put up with it to persevere. Seeing as it stopped bleeding and I couldn't get time off work that's exactly what I did. After turning back into a lump it remained settled for several years. One night while I was laying in bed I could smell a terrible odour creeping up from under my blankets.

At that very moment I had to scratch into the top of my bum crack. To my surprise the hole had re appeared and it was itchy. Boy it smelled bad and silky stuff was coming out of it onto my fingers. It smelled like a rotting corpse so I made an appointment to have it removed but this time they said it was a sinus. I was scheduled for surgery but once again the hole closed over but they seem to have removed the gland. The surgeons cut into the area where the suspected sinus was but said they never found anything.

CHAPTER 4

Police Special

A job for someone to run 300 acres of turf was advertised in the paper. Although I had been cutting turf and loading turf trucks for about 4 years I didn't have the necessary experience required. I applied anyway as it was the only job In the paper I knew anything about. Needing a reference I went to see John Farlane. John Farlane owned the turf farm just up the road and I had been working on and off for him since I was 13. John wasn't home he was away fishing. John had a obsession with black fish and would take off without notice and no one would know when he would return. Sensing I really wanted the job his son said he would pretend he was his dad and write the reference for me. "show me the newspaper add" he said. He wanted to address all the things they were looking for and put it into the reference. Before you knew it according to the reference I was an expert in all aspects of turf farming and I got the job. "you'll be right just come and ask us about anything your unsure of" John Farlanes son said when he handed me the reference but from what the people that owned the turf farm had said I would need to know everything. I couldn't believe how good he made me look. The turf farm was run down and hadn't operated in over 15 years. I had no idea what I was in for but everything fell into place bit by bit and piece by piece. All the machinery was broken and the turf itself was couch and was dead and full of weeds. Couch dies in the winter or when it has no nutrients. It can remain dormant for years then be revived but this stuff was mostly weeds. The farm had had that many layers cut out of it that it needed top dressing every paddock to bring it back up to scratch. Unfortunately that wasn't a option as the owners didn't have millions of dollars to put into the farm so I had to work with what I had. Lucky for me there were no orders for turf the week I started and most of the tractors and machinery problems were just blown hydraulic hoses and easily fixed by my father. My father was a boss in the coal mines but used to be a diesel fitter. He got most of the parts he needed from the mine itself. Within a week They started taking orders and had hired a old guy with a small truck to deliver the turf but all he wanted to do was talk and stand around. 3 weeks later I bought a brand-new medium size truck and had convinced the owners that my brother would be better suited to deliver the turf. That way no one could see how hopeless I was at cutting the stuff, no one that could tell the owners anyway. Cutting turf is a tricky thing to do as it takes a precise measurement or layer of dirt to be able to get it to roll. All turf comes in rolls and is a strip of grass approximately ten feet long by one and a half feet wide that is rolled up. The root system Of the grass is supposed to mat the layer of dirt together so it can be rolled up but this stuff was completely dead. At first I thought of cutting it with a thicker amount of dirt but the more dirt the heavier the rolls were and they became too heavy to lift. After a while of trial and error I worked it out. I worked out that if I wet the ground the night before then pulled a giant roller over it I could get it to roll If I cut the dirt layer wafer thin. That way it could bend easier and made really small light rolls. The trouble with that was by the time the rolls got to there destination they had all broken apart as the dirt would dry and crumble and you had to pretty much shovel it off the truck. We had nothing but complaints. Complaints about the quality of the grass, the quality of the rolls and the weeds but again I was lucky as the owners told me it wasn't my fault. It didn't seem to matter as the owners turned out to be very shrewd business people. Sandra the owner owned Australian turf before it became Australian native landscapes. She owned farms all over Windsor. Sandra was now a fashion designer and owned shops in the

Queen Victoria building. She knew business and it wouldnt be long before the reasons why she wanted to revamp a old worn out turf farm were clear. The daughter in-law worked in with councils and football clubs and was extremely good looking. She could work her way into anything. Before we knew it Wahroonga shire council had signed the farm to a contract. The contract was to turf all of the football and soccer fields around the Manly and Deewhy areas along with all of the foreshores and parks and gardens. It was almost as if they new in advance. We were churning it out 25,000 square feet a day with just me and my best mate Paul cutting it. We worked really hard and it was non stop work from 6am until dark. Someone was now needed to lay the turf so I employed 3 casuals and excepted the contract to not only cut it and deliver it but lay the turf down as well. Life was good I was clearing $3000 a week in 1987 but working 7 14 hour days for it. Smally one of the guys I had employed to lay the turf carried a shotgun everywhere he went. Smally carried it everywhere whenever he left the house and everyone knew he did this. They were laying turf and camping down the city on the football grounds with a shotgun at all times occasionally shooting at the birds. They laid the turf you see in home and away with a shotgun in hand its unbelievable but its true. It wasn't just any shotgun either it was a Winchester Police Special. Only the police had access to these guns as they were shorter then other shotguns and clip into the boot of the police cars. Craig had a friend that was a gun smith and he obtained the gun for Smally. You would think he would have carried a pistol so he could conceal it better if he had those sort of connections. Some time after I had finished turfing and was working in the mines Smally rang and asked did I still hire the truck out with a driver and offered to pay me decent money. He said he needed a truck and driver for about 4 hours work and that he would fill me in on the details when I picked him up. Used to him carrying the shotgun at all times I didn't think anything suspicious when he loaded it into my cab. "Get in Smally" I said when I picked him up. "im right with the shotty aint I" he said also joking it was part of the job to carry it. If he had of told me straight away what he was about to do I wouldnt have driven him anywhere. "To Penrith" he instructed so off I drove.

Along the way he told me we had to move some furniture of his girlfriends and that she worked in Penrith so again I never suspected anything. Once at Penrith he got me to park up for about 20 minutes saying we had to follow the girlfriend home to her place then move the furniture. Once he saw the girlfriend get in the car we followed her to a house near Campbelltown and he got me to park across the road. It was late afternoon just before the streetlights were to come on. "what now" I asked and he replied "he'll be here in a minute you watch". I asked who will be here in a minute and he told me to watch and a silver ford station wagon will pull up, a guy will get out and the bedroom lights will go on. He was right that's exactly what happened. Next thing Smally grabs his shotgun and jumps out of the truck. "bang bang bang bang bang" he pounded on the door "open up its the police" he shouted. All of a sudden the door opened and a woman screamed "arhhhh arrhhh please Smally no she pleaded. Next minute I hear a guy yell out "oh my god" then jump out the window with no clothes on and crouch down behind a car right in front of me. Smally has then come out of the house and started smashing the shotgun butt into the guys car until the butt snapped clean off it. As he started approaching the truck I started up the engine and the guy hiding ran down the road. People started coming out of there houses onto the street so I left my lights off and got out of there fast as I could. I wasn't happy as he could easily have had me charged with accessory to murder if he had of shot the bloke and as it was accessory to home invasion is bad enough. I cursed and swore at him but it was too late there was nothing I could do that would change anything. All I could do is try and make sure I got out of there un noticed. To this day Smally has never paid me for driving the truck.

CHAPTER 5

Aida Rose

I was born in 1969. It was the year man walked on the moon. Growing up I spent lots of time at the beach or in the back yard and pool. My father was a workaholic. He worked full shifts in the coal mines then came home and continued working up to 7 hours building our house. He would build by himself and he built every day. Before I was born he bought a tiny 3 room dwelling in Georges avenue, one street over from Bulli pass. As I was growing up he turned it into a 2 story place with a pool, pergola and barbecue area. Both my mum and dad were great parents. Although they worked many hours they had plenty of time for me and the older brother Wayne. They must have never slept. I remember our adventures in dads Holden Hr Ute. We travelled the escarpment overlooking Wollongong into water board and national parks. Area similar to that of the blue mountains. He would get large pieces of sandstone for the garden. He would grab a cold chisel and hammer, then chisel into the fault lines in the rock breaking off huge slabs and somehow he would manoeuvre them into the back of his Ute. He was really strong, only a small man but one of the strongest men I've ever known. He can pick up his boat and trailer and walk it to the car. I can only just pick up the boat. Everything regarding my parents and my upbringing was rosey. Our relationship was perfect until my grandmother died. My grandmother had blue hair and when I was a boy I thought she was the queen of England. She owned newspaper stands all throughout Sydney and her father owned newspaper stands at saint James train station. My nan and pop on my mother's side said Grandma was important so I really did think she was the queen. For as long as I remember I saw her every second Sunday until in my late twenty's. We would sit all day and she would tell me story's. her memory was impeccable. She remembered what year things happened and the month or if she didn't know she could always work it out. My father however had a unusual relationship with her. He didn't call her mum he called her stupid. That's what he called her. He would say "what are you on about stupid". It seemed my dad blamed her for his father leaving when he was 11. I'm sure that's why he did what he did as he didn't know at the time she was giving her estate to me. Although he called her stupid he did look after her and would go mow her lawns when she got old. On one of those occasions she asked my father to recite her last wishes. "what for stupid why would I do that" he replied. "it's important to me Mark please say it" she said but he refused. Grandma said "go against my wishes Mark, mark my words I'll haunt you". She turned to me and asked me to say her last wishes so I started to recite the wishes she had told me. "The artery's in both arms and legs are to be severed and the blood drained from your body, this is to ensure that you died as you have a fear of being buried alive. Your body is to be buried not cremated, its to go back into the ground from which it came and you're to be buried at forest lawn cemetery Bringelly new south Wales. Finally the house at Kingsgrove was not to be sold to the wog next door. Just after that she gave out 3 large white bibles each containing a copy of her last wishes. She gave one to my dad, his brother and my brother also received one. At the time I thought it was strange I didn't get a copy but now it's clear it's because I already knew. I guess she trusted me to remember and to see her wishes through. Before she died in 1999 my father took power of attorney and stopped me from seeing my grandmother. He did this by making out she was crazy. She used to say the Wog was stealing the palings off the fence and the Wog next door was stealing iron off the roof. She also accused him of stealing bricks she had stashed under the house. My grandmother was a bit of a hoarder. She had enough materials to build another house. The Wog next door made my father offers to buy the house 8 or 9 years before she died as he and his brother had been buying houses in the street. They started off with one house. Both brothers lived with there wives in one while they built it into a mansion. After a while both had children and needed another house so they bought a house across the road and built on top of it. Now they were buying other houses in the street for there son's. My grandmother had seen him checking the footings to see if it had sound foundations and she would think he was stealing the bricks that were stacked under the house. She caught him checking the roof to see if it needed replacing and she thought he was stealing the iron from off the roof. She also caught him checking the fences and thought the palings were missing. My dad used that to make her look delusional but I pointed out to my father that she was sane. When checking the fence the wog found the fence was in the wrong place and my grandmother had to pay half to have a new fence put in. I explained she must have seen him checking it and thought he was stealing palings "she's not crazy" I pointed out. He wouldn't listen and took power of attorney and changed her will. I remember my grandfather while they were selling her other house one time. They were selling it on her as they thought she had no money for food. Centrelink only gave her 18 dollars a week as she had too many assets. My grandfather whilst driving to the tip started saying "she's giving all her money away Mark". My father said she was giving 5 % to the church. Grandfather said "no she's not giving it to the church but trust me she's giving it away". Grandfather then asked which son I was, was I the oldest boy or the youngest. "the youngest" my father said. He then told dad they should talk when alone. I only saw my grandfather twice a year once on my birthday and on boxing day after Christmas so I can understand he didn't know which one I was. On these boxing day occasions both grandparents were as if they were married. It was bazaar as he had another wife but would come and see grandmother every year. Grandma had forbid my parents allowing his wife to see us kids and she threatened if they broke this rule she would cast them out of the will. My parents had broken this rule many times. To cut the long story short my father put grandmother in a home. He did that 8 years before she died and I never seen her again. All I would hear is story's of how she would fall down at my father's feet and beg him to take her home calling him master. "Please take me home" she would beg. When she died I was in Queensland so my father rushed the funeral and had her cremated. Cremation wasn't supposed to happen as she was to go into the ground from which she came and that is what her last wishes said. He also sold the house to the Wog next door. Both myself and my brother were in disbelief when he told us on the phone. We objected but there was nothing we could do. Grandma was cremated and her ashes buried with her parents and still today 21 years later there's no plaque with Aida Rose Hickey saying she is there. My father and I were underground coal miners he retired at 52. He did have a massive heart attack around the time and the mine he worked at had closed but It wasn't the heart attack or closure that stopped him working. He received enough money from grandmother's estate that there was no need to return to work. He was a boss at work and didn't really do much if he didn't want to. This started a fued between us. At the time it hadn't even dawned on me my grandmother intended leaving me everything. I was just angry my father had gone against her wishes and I had seriously considered contesting the will. Knowing this my father set out to destroy me so I couldn't fund a legal action. At the time of grandma's death I worked for SBD mining services, ready workforce and Mastermyne. At that time work for me in the mines was only contract and usually temporary. That suited me. I loved time off as I had no mortgages or car repayments and could go periods without work. It was good having no responsibilities and before I knew it I was back in Rockhampton. I had forgot about grandma as I was back on the drugs which I loved very much. There was a rumour spreading through criminals in Rockhampton. The rumour was I was a undercover cop as I was from Sydney and new to the drug scene there. When I worked in the mines I'd be staying in towns 700klms away. On my days off I often drove to Rockhampton to buy drugs and stay in motels. Rocky Is a isolated town of 90,000 people. it's like one big tight knit kind of place where everyone knows everyone. I say related as police are related to the criminals and the criminals related to the prison guards and lawyers. They all went to school together and so on. The crims in Rockhampton didn't know me from a bar of soap. They didn't know me and I didn't want them knowing me I just needed to score drugs. I've worked and scored drugs all over the country but these crims turned out the best scammers I've ever seen. Often I would get ripped off. When I say ripped off it would be the drugs but half would be missing. "That's alright" I would think you can't expect them to do something for nothing so I would pull out more money and go again. I had no other option as I needed that amount. I was clearing after tax take home pay on average $1600 in 2002. That's for 4 days on and 4 days off. The most I cleared was $1780 for 3 days work. I was hired out by ready workforce as specialized labour. They paid $29 per hour for the first 8 hours then $50 for every hour after plus $70 a day bonus. The fact I could hand them 5-700 cash get ripped and pull out more made them suspicious and they would think I must be a cop trying to find stuff out. The cop theory would remain until the present day. I guess I'll never shake it as part of who I was even after serving 13 prison tours at Capricorn correction centre my closest mates were still suspicious I was a undercover cop. The cop theory was brought about by simple things I did. I would say I didn't want to know anyone when they wanted to introduce me. They thought it was reverse psychology. Id be there one minute then disappear for weeks and sometimes I had a goat beard, sometimes a moustache, other times the full beard. This all made them suspicious so they took it upon themselves to investigate. To do this they used a woman called Sheridan or Tinkerbelle as she is known. Tinkerbelle was a middle man and like half the middle men in rocky she had heard of me and heard the story's. Uncle Norman was one of the main dealers in rocky. He had got her to find out what I was about. "If he's a cop Tinkerbelle will flush him out" Norman would have thought. At the time I was actually glad to meet Tinkerbelle as she seemed down the line with me and straight forward. I told her how much I needed for my days off and I told her what I'd do is buy one package I could share with her then buy another for myself, plus id give her $50 cash. I did this if she charged what they charged her and the size was right. Buying grams was small fry I bought ounces just for personal use. Knowing Norman wanted to know me she said "I'll introduce you to Norman" "you can see him yourself" I honestly didn't want to meet anyone else as So far everyone was a bit of a asshole you wouldn't want to meet. She told me Norman wanted to know me and so did a lot of other people. To be honest I was frightened of them. I was frightened of the story's I would hear. A lot of these people had been to prison and that scared me. Years earlier I had met a guy called Tony Bent. Tony used to run a big section of long bay jail. He'd been in Parramatta prison when the riots were on. He seemed nice enough but scared the hell out of me with things he done and did. He had just served 17 years for double murder and he'd been in prison since he was 17. There was nothing he was scared of. I first met him on weekend release. He served 16 of his 17 years so there was no risk of him escaping and they had transferred him to park lea correctional centre for low risk and young offenders. Before I knew it I was talked into taking heroin to the prison. It was ridiculous I didn't know the guy I had met him once at my dealers place. I would seriously questioned his interests in my 17 year old fiancée. She was worried he might try and rape her as he had showed her lots of attention and compliments. I had never been to a prison before and now I had heroin in caps taped to the drawstring in my jacket. I was to pull the string and hand it to him during what they call a family visit. I was there with a mate and his girlfriend and we had 2 barbecued chooks. The chickens had weed shoved up them and the seasoning stuffed back in. Yes you could take in chickens back in those days. I did ask why we didn't put heroin in the chickens and they said they don't like the drugs together incase it gets busted. "you will lose the lot" they said. No-one told me I needed identification. I didn't have a driver's license and needed my birth certificate as they stopped me from going through to the visits. I quickly rang my father and got him to drive half way from Oakdale. While dad drove one way I drove the mates van the other way to meet him. I then raced back but again the guards stopped me even though visits still had 15 minutes. The screws that organized my dad agreed to let me through once they had the identification but they must have sensed the urgency and knew there was drugs as they wouldnt let me through. That still worked though as It drew attention away from the drugs in the chickens. Tony Dent was apparently proud of me and he was happy about the effort I had gone to. The day he got released I received a phone call "be out front in 10 minutes" the person said also saying "Tony will be there to pick you up". I said "who the fuck is Tony". They repeated themselves and asked if I was sure I didn't know a Tony" "perhaps one that just served 17 years" the person said. He was coming to pay his respects which I thought strange and I still think he was after my fiancée. Once I knew who it was I couldn't say no so I went and waited at the mail box. Tony had over the course of running long bay and Silverwater jail looked after some pretty notorious people. Some were brothel owners, some were drug dealers and some were rich socialites. He turned up with 20 thousand dollars worth of heroin. Payment for looking after the owner of a chain of brothels from kings cross to Campbelltown. He had the heroin and a couple of roscoes in the car. At first I thought roscoe was the name for the automatic weapon he was carrying. Now I know roscoe is what the criminals call a gun. I hopped into the car with the convicted murderer knowing he had killed the 2 men at 17 with his hands. He had broke both there necks. "Where to" he asked and I laughed "but your the one picking me up" I said. "What is it you want Tony" "why have you come to see me" I asked. he showed me the 20 grand ball of heroin it was larger then a golf ball. Anyone who knows pure heroin knows a match head size rock kills 2 or 3 people that didn't have a habit. "Im here to shout you a shot and a party on the heroin" he said. We needed a spot where we couldn't be disturbed so I told the driver to turn around and head back the way he came. Then I told Tony about johns house and how the house was over grown with black berry bushes. You couldn't see It from the road. "You may have to give him some heroin" I told Tony who asked if I owed him anything? Tony said John wasn't getting anything unless he paid. I told Tony it was his house but Tony didn't care saying "where Tony goes Tony rules" "you'll see" he said. He was right John begged and begged for heroin but Tony wouldn't give it to him but after saying I would pay the money he eventually gave in. John was the kind that would say anything he had to to get heroin so I had to explain that he needed to pay this time as

Tony had already given threats. The trouble was he meant every word he said. If he says he'll burn ya house down then I'm sure he will burn your house down. We partied for a couple of days until Tony made up for what Id done. The whole time he kept on asking me about my Colorado boots. Tony was 6 ft 4 and had about a size 15 shoe. He eventually managed to get a pair, he just took them he said and laughed. Where he'd come from if you like someone's shoes you take them if you can. In prison weaker guys get there shoes taken by stronger guys it's a very un-civilized place. After a few days Tony had gone from giving me heroin to selling me heroin in small prison sizes. In Cabramatta I could get it for half the price of Tony's but if I did that Tony would know. Heroin is something you need daily. If you didn't buy from Tony he would tell you he knew you bought it from someone else. He made our world's as if we were in prison. That was ok we managed. Tony and his ball of heroin couldn't last long and although it got hard and the price went up it eventually ran out. Tony had reverted into the back room of a friends house. He had a old desk in there and he never left that room and It seemed he was institutionalized quite severely. He sat in there 8 weeks until the heroin ran out. After the heroin was gone he started doing arm robs by himself. He would do things like car jack some innocent lady and keep her hostage and make her drive. Now the heroin was gone I hardly saw him. One time he came to borrow money I remember it clearly. The way he asked was different to anything I've ever witnessed "ya going to lend me 200 bucks and I'll pay you back in 3 days time" he said. I told him I had $250 and $100 had to go to my father but he said "your not hearing me" listen carefully "your lending me 200 and I'll pay it back in 3 days" "either that or I take it but then I might not give it back" so I lent it to him and it came back 3 days later. The next time I seen Tony he pulled off a large jewellery heist. He did it with a guy he knew from prison as this guy had a rich aunty that was a actress or so I was told. She had all her rings and necklaces in the walls for safe keeping. Some old people are really smart about how they stash there valuables. We knew a guy called Ibrah from looking after brothel owners. Underbelly was right Ibrah didn't make his money from drugs. Although they didn't know how he got his money I can tell you its from gold and diamonds. What he did was buy any gold rings. Rings either stolen or off people hanging out for drugs and he would then melt it down. He would get all the diamonds and sapphires for free saying "I don't want the diamonds I just want the gold" telling them they could pull them out themselves and handing them a pair of pliers. 90% of junkies were in too much of a hurry and would take the $9 per gram. If you ever tried to pull out a tiny diamond from a ring you would know Its pretty hard to do. Ibrah used to run the service station at Currans hill near Narellan so we went to see him about the jewellery. From what I was told they were talking around half a million dollars worth of stuff. Ibrah said he owned a night club in kings cross and that It would be easier to have the jewellery inspected there he said. That way the buyer and the seller could meet in his back room and Both could feel secure as he had big security guards. Tony agreed to do that so we went and waited to go that night. Tony in the meantime swapped some of the smaller diamond rings. He unloaded them cheap as he had plenty of jewellery. 5 hours later and we were in kings cross. Tony gave us a pep talk "There's 4 of us, as long as we stick together and didn't drink much we'll get through this with biggest pay day of our lives" Tony wasn't concerned about being robbed as he had a hand gun. From memory it could have been a 22. Steve had a hand made 22 handgun with a silencer I'm not sure if it was the same one. I just remember Tony planting the gun down on the white table in the back room. There was a jeweller sitting across from Tony ready to inspect everything. The jeweller asked about the heist as he was concerned it would be red hot and he was worried about police. police may not have been notified at that stage but I don't remember the details. Tony told of how these necklaces had giant ruby's and other gems hanging from them and he said the stones were huge. He reached into the bag that had the semi automatic and pulled out a huge necklace and threw it to the jeweller. The jeweller looked shocked and said "I'm looking for something more elegant, something smaller" and laughed. Tony laughed until the jeweller threw it back "the real ones please" "this is no time for games" he said. Tony had a heap of costume jewellery actresses wore in the theatre. There were real diamond rings and probably about

30,000 dollars worth but Tony had traded them off for $4000 worth of heroin. Some were sold for weight in gold to Ibrah at his Curran's hill service station. Tony felt like a dickhead but it was a easy mistake for him to make. He had spent his entire life in prison and never seen real jewellery before. I never saw Tony again for about 4 months. He was on a train heading towards Cabramatta and it was before he got caught for the armed robs. He was completely broke and I shouted him some drugs for old time sake. He explained to me to never go to prison I was too nice. The inmates would take from me all day I was told. He explained everything you own fits into a 4ft by 3ft plastic tub and that most of that was your clothing and bedding and owned by the prison. All you owned in the world were little things like matches or a deck of cards. Cards and maybe a book or two he said. If someone borrowed 40 of your 50 matches it was a big chunk of everything you owned. If he didn't give it back you would have to smash his head in like your fighting to the death. At 22 I wasn't the type to fight. I was when I was bit younger as I used to bash my older brother and his mates at high school no problem but I developed a form epilepsy at 17. I often thought it was the medication that caused me to get knocked out. I remembered getting easily beaten by a weaker opponent and knocked unconscious. Being knocked off my feet was humiliating so I made sure that wasn't going to happen again. By 30 I was sick and tired of being stood over and told I was wrong when I was right. It got to the point I'd had enough and started boxing twice a day. Now I was stuck in Rockhampton. I was scared of local criminals especially if they'd been to prison. I had a friend that lived next door to my brother. He new some of the criminals and that's as close as I wanted to get to them. I now had tinkerbells phone number. Before I'd leave the miners camp and drive the 700klms I would ring Sheridan to let her know I was coming. The fact I would drive 700klms in 4 hours added to the theory I was a undercover cop. Tinkerbelle tried to stick to me like glue but I could always escape to work. One time she managed to stay with me in a motel. Whilst I was asleep she took my car keys and drove my car. She drove it to uncle Normans house and there they all investigated my personal things. In the boot was a briefcase full of photo identification for the mines and on these cards the company name was written as co name VLD. Some of the other names were co name SBD. I always looked different so naturally the crims thought I was a cop. They thought because it said SBD the D Stood for detective. Co name stood for company name but to them it meant code name and they pegged me for a cop. I had caught wind of the rumours through my brothers next door neighbour. I thought whilst it put me in huge amounts of danger it also kept me safe. They would have to be stupid to mess with me if I was a cop like they were saying. I'd finished the mining contract I was working and headed to Mackay. I met up with a secretary that worked for the same company. I hit it off with Charmaine the first time we spoke over the phone and I remember her saying my start dates and what mine I'd be working at. She said who to see when I turned up on site and she said I needed a drug test and to give a clean urine. "yeah that's fine I don't smoke marijuana" I told her and she laughed and said thanks for your honesty and from that single conversation I was intrigued. I loved the sound of her voice. To me although I had no idea what she looked like I was sure she was good-looking. Over time I got to talk to her quite regularly and I had deliberately got her to split my pay into 2 different accounts. She did it weekly so I had a excuse to ring the office as I had to tell her what to put in the other account each week. We would chat all the time and soon I found she rang me during the day whilst I was sleeping after night shift. I eventually said some things that lead to us meeting in Mackay. I asked for pants to be made with the zipper running sideways instead of up and down. "why" Charmaine asked. I told her that's because of the belt that holds my tools and cap lamp battery as I can't undue my zipper to go to the toilet. She laughed and said "how are you off for sox and underpants" I then said "why are you going to send me a pair of yours" "ooowah" she said and slammed the phone down hanging up on me. I panicked myself sick thinking oh my god what have I done. I stressed about it for about a hour and then rang to apologize. To my surprise she said it was actually a bit of a turn on so I asked if I should take her out for dinner or straight to the motel. As soon as I got to Mackay I went to a motel and rang her with the room number and about a hour later she turned up. she wasn't at all like I had imagined. I imagined a brunette with past the shoulders length hair, not tall but not short, A Nice slim build with a hot ass and that secretary look. She was blonde and quite short. She's wasn't ugly and had a nice body just not the girl I had imagined. It was ok I was in love with her anyway. We had sex and a cigarette and just snuggled. I asked if she wanted to go somewhere and have some dinner but she was happy to stay there she said. She was tired and so was I and we slept from 6pm right round. I woke once during the night but never turned or moved. It was the most satisfying sleep I had had in a long time. In the morning I got up and had a shower. I woke her asking her was she going to have a shower. "not to get into the same clothes" she said "saying she may as well go home and shower and get changed there. I walked her to her car and kissed her. "where do we go from here" I said. "again it's your call" she said "I'm not going anywhere". I told her I was going to Sydney to see my son but would be back in about 2 weeks. Sooner if another contract starts. I asked her to keep her ear out for more work then promised I'd be in touch. She left and I rang Tinkerbelle as I needed some speed for the drive to Sydney. I jumped in my car and drove the 300 Klms to Rockhampton. The drive from Mackay to Rockhampton was a 3 hour trip but if you drove at 170 you can get there in 2 so that's exactly what I used to do. I didn't have a license I never ever had a license in my life so there was nothing to lose. The closest I ever came to a license was a learners permit which I lost when I was 18 for high-speed pursuits. Back then driving without a license was only a $400 fine you didn't actually get in trouble. There was no disqualification period from the courts and you rarely got pulled over if doing the right thing. The drive from Mackay to Rockhampton is long open stretches of straight road 170 kilometres per hour was nothing everyone drove like that. If you passed a police car coming the other way you just accelerate faster and by the time he has turned around to give chase you've built up a good lead. It's not something you go to prison for the first time and I've out run the police plenty of times before. I've also been caught and my criminal record is long and dated back to when I was 15 years old. I got my first charges for assault police, resist arrest, hinder arrest and incite a riot after a high speed pursuit.

My brother was in one car and myself in another with a girl driving. When the police finally caught us I started fighting in front of a crowd of people. We were at a eurogliders concert. They never actually caught us running. we were headed to the concert and had merely stopped. I ended up getting my leg and knee cap busted with the riot batten. The brother and I learnt a valuable lesson in respect for authority and to this day I've never resisted again. I'm a yes sir no sir 3 bags full sir kind of guy. Tell them my name date of birth and address then nothing after that. You just tell them your details and then say no comment from then on. You don't have to come up with a bullshit story and it's better not to as the bullshit will get you busted for something and you'll be charged for that as well. 2 hours after I rang Sheridan and told her I was leaving Mackay I arrived in Rockhampton. I knew they thought I was a cop but it was about to get much worse. I actually did work with Jay fisher. We worked side by side day in and day out and his wife was a under cover cop. He used to let me in on secrets about her undercover operations. I picked up Sheridan so we could go score some drugs. When she rang uncle Norman the heat was on he said. That means he thought police were coming and he needed to get out of where he was and fast. Sheridan told him she was with me and for some reason he asked could we pick him up. It spins me out how these criminals take drugs then think police are coming all the time. They also think they can hide out and the cops won't find them. if the police want you bad enough they'll find you. I couldn't see the point in being scared of what may be as being scared never saved anybody from being caught. In fact being scared in some cases will get you in trouble and get you caught. You can tell when someone's hiding something if they're nervous. It's common sense so I enjoy myself with what I'm doing and if that means breaking the law then I make sure I enjoy that while I'm doing it. After all that's what your taking the drugs for in the first place. After consideration I agreed to pick up Norman. I didn't want to meet him I wanted his drugs so I really didn't have a choice. Norman was about 49 or 50 years old. I had imagined some big staunch fella but he was older and had a lot of character. He had lots of gold. Norman had a ring on almost every finger and they were unusual rings the kind you can only obtain if they were hand made. Some had sapphires in them. I knew sapphires came from near Rockhampton as I had a girlfriend that lived out the gem fields. The gem fields or ruby vale was out past emerald and the coal mines. It was probably Australia's richest sapphire deposits. There were thousands of holes in the ground some abandon private leases in the middle of nowhere and would be a ideal spot to get rid of a body. You never hear of police ever searching abandon mine shafts. Never in Australian history as far as I'm aware. Police never inspected the mines for missing people. The same went for the underground coal mines which would be even easier to dispose of someone. In the coal mines they have a area called the goaf and that area is always rumoured to be full of ghosts "Pye whys" the old miners used to call them. What happens underground is they tunnel 3 road ways in the same direction. Each roadway is 50 metres apart. They might tunnel each road way for 500 metres and every 50 metres down the road way would be a road way side ways. That road cuts across to other roadways and its called a cut through. This formed giant square blocks of coal all the way to the end of the 500 metre roadway. Then once all the road ways and square blocks of coal were formed they would work backwards from the end of the roadways and mine out all the coal. Once the coal was gone you are left with nothing holding up the roof. There is a giant area at times the size of 6 football fields with nothing holding it up. It has to fall down so millions of tonnes of rock crash down on top of anything left there. Police would never be able to look there even if they had a strong suspicion there were body's, it's impossible. Depending on what mine your in the coal seam is between 1 to 3 kilometres below the surface. It would cost billions of dollars and be impossible to remove the broken strata out of the way. Anyway, I liked Normans rings. The guys out the gem fields I had met used to have the nicest gold rings. Rings with sapphires in them. Blue and yellow or party coloured sapphires. Normans looked hand crafted not mass produced like from a jeweller. I was thinking Norman must know people from out the gem fields because of his rings. I was thinking I could end up in hole. I always used to think the worst case scenario and work my way backwards but my motto was "don't let fear stop you" like I said before being scared won't save you but being aware just might. At least I now had something to talk to the man about. I asked about the rings and was right. He collected gold trinkets and sapphires so I swapped him some my girlfriend gave me. I swapped him the stones for little viles of pethadine that he had. My girlfriend had given me the stones and said they weren't much good so I told him that. He didn't mind and gave me the pethadine anyway as a gesture of goodwill. He didn't have any speed because he was worried about the cops. Someone had caused his concern I can't remember what it was exactly. He thought police were coming for him so we had taken him to Roy Trifford's house to hide out. I don't know why as Roy Trifford was also a drug dealer that worked for uncle Norman. Police aren't stupid they would have known this and It would be the first place they would look. Roy was known to be a close associate of Normans. We organized to get my 8 ball the following day so I could drive to Sydney. We did so on the condition that I brought Norman back some heroin. When he mentioned heroin it dawned on me that I had met him ten years earlier "I thought you looked familiar" I said mentioning that I used to be on the methadone program in Rockhampton. I had met him at the clinic and scored heroin from him out Gracemere. Gracemere was a town not far away from Rockhampton. After jolting his memory told us how police had let him out of prison giving him $10,000 worth of heroin and a plane ticket. I got the impression Roy Trifford didn't like that I was getting on with Norman. He never said anything but perhaps he thought I was moving to fast or was a threat to his position selling drug. I had just cut out the middle men as Norman gave me his number. Roy had pulled me to the side and warned me about Sheridan. He was saying she was trouble and to watch out for her. She would fuck me over he said but I thought he was trying to cause trouble and never listened. Sheridan and I left and I went to my ex girlfriends brothers for the night. I went there to wait as I couldn't leave without the drugs. It was too long a drive to Sydney without it. In the morning I rang Norman and he was out at the beach at a town called Yeppoon and he asked if I could meet him out there. I took the ex girlfriends brother with me as I was still a little frightened of these people thinking I was a cop. The beach meant boats and to me the ocean was another perfect spot to try dispose of me. I know it seems silly to think like that but it's kept me safe all these years. I went to the beach to meet Norman but where he told me to wait was a car with purely electronics on the side of it. In the car was a guy in the car had a camera so I went to a payphone and rang Norman. I told him not to meet us there and I met him somewhere else. Norman was happy that I actually cared saying "most junkies wouldn't have noticed enough to warn me" "they would just want the drugs". After returning to Rockhampton I prepared to leave but I wanted to check in with Sheridan first. Tinkerbell had just been hit multiple times round the ribs with a baseball bat and it was obvious she had people trying to hurt her. I was frightened for Sheridan so I checked and made sure she was ok. When she answered she said police were everywhere looking for her and she was hiding just up the road from them watching there flashing lights. She couldn't escape on foot "can you come and pick me up" she said. She described roughly where she was so I got in the car from Simpson's motel and headed over the bridge towards Amart All Sports. As I was heading up the dual laneway there was a booze bus and Police had just let 3 cars go. Damn it I thought as they pull 3 cars over each time and I was car number 3 in the line. Police waved down the first car and I had slowed down to 10 Klms below the speed limit. They waved down the second car and I knew I was gone as there was no avoiding it. There was a 4th car gaining behind but it was to late I thought. I had just put my blinker on to pull over as the police were stepping out to wave me in. The car behind sped up and overtook me and pulled in in my place. I couldn't believe it. I drove up to a street on the left and turned into it. It was opposite to where I thought Sheridan was hiding and there was a phone box so I rang Sheridan and told her where I was. "shit no"" that's just up from the police and where there looking for me" she said. I told Sheridan it was just a booze bus. It took a while to get the message through to her though but I said "why would they be looking for you? She was just delusional on the drugs and probably hadn't slept in days. The mind plays tricks on you when your really tired. I coaxed her around to realizing police had no reason to manhunt for her and She walked across the road and got into my car.

Within seconds she had totally forgot the whole 2 hour ordeal. She was now on her usual mission of getting drugs out of me. She remembered I had to meet with Norman and pick some up. I decided to stay the night and actually sleep. I convinced her she may as well stay in the motel with me. She wasn't a oil painting but she wasn't ugly and at times she use to try make it look like we were together. I think she wanted to be and the fact we weren't disappointed her. That night we went to sleep as what I had gotten off Norman wasn't that good and wasn't worth the wait. Sheridan talked about calliope a town about 120klms south of Rockhampton. She said the gear there was something special but you had to buy about 750 dollars worth. She made a phone call and apparently the guy was holding some for us. She asked did I still have money left and I said enough to get me through but I wasn't sure how long another job would be. She said it's ok and that she could turn 750 into 1500 if I wanted to hang around. I would have to play Sheridan's game though she said and laughed. I had no idea why they called her Tinkerbelle but I guess I'd soon find out.

CHAPTER 6

The Mecca

The permanent underground miners and all c,f,m,e,u union members were on strike. I was a union member a Oakey creek lodge member. I talked to Lee Beckart the owner of Mastermyne which was the contract mining company I worked for. He talked to us about what to do if working that day as we were on casual contract. breaching the contract would mean big fines as a penalty for Mastermyne. That would affect the amount of bonus us men would make and probably mean we made no bonus at all. Lee said if we didn't turn up for work the company would be held for breach of contract, a fine of $50,000 would be imposed and they would be sued. He said he understood some of us were union members. He told us it was ok if we didn't want to work and instead strike with the other members. Lee went on to say all we had to do was turn up for work. if there was a picket line of demonstrators and we felt intimidated or couldn't cross the picket line because we felt we were in danger the company would be legally ok. The contract says the mining company must provide a safe environment for us to work in at all times he said "so it's simple just turn up then go home if your intimidated or feel endangered". He was a very smart man, it's easy to see why he and his company were so successful. We turned up and to our surprise there was no union picket line at the gate like we were expecting. We were expecting demonstrators. There was nothing to cause us any danger. Working while my colleagues were on strike bothered me I had been on strike many times when I was permanent and we increased the rate of pay and working conditions that we had. The only time it was ethical to ever work whilst on strike was when the union told some of the miners to work while the others go on strike. the ones working could sacrifice 20 percent of there pay each week and the union could pay it to the members out on strike. that way the strikers could afford to pay there mortgages and strike longer being more effective. It worked as it caused the mining company's to lose money and they would agree to give us what we wanted. I didn't want my reputation to be tarnished as a scab so I talked to our shift boss Dick Lock. Dick decided that we should all go underground. There was now a official record of us signing on. The mining company records that you are at work when you pick up your cap lamp, gas monitor and machine for day. Once we were underground we could have a meeting. Dick Lock said at the meeting we were to have underground. "Anyone worried or thought there reputations would be injured then they could go home". We turned off the main road into the particular section we were to be working and had our meeting. Jim leak used to be a permanent employee. He was also a staunch union member at one stage "fuck the union" He said trying as hard as he could to talk us into working. I spoke up for the union. I pointed out that Jim leak was just angry because the union couldn't save his job. Jim had punched one of the bosses in the face. Everyone knew that was a instant dismissal case and there was nothing the union could do. I made a few solid points and Jim leak said "fuck off demo" "when's the union ever helped you" he said saying "you tell me when the union has ever saved anyone's job". I took a deep breath and thought for a second. I didn't actually know of anyone except me. I told the blokes my story about the mining company Clutha trying to sack me for drugs. Drugs and not going to work for 38 days. The union stepped in and saved my job at the eleventh hour. We didn't work we sat down in the rib. The rib is the side walls, The sides and where the sidewalls meet the floor. It is made of crumbled coal which makes a ideal place to sit. We sat down and the blokes started talking there usual chit chat. Bill was saying "so what did ya do on the weekend Robert" and Robert told of how he mowed the lawn and took the kids to soccer and after that had a huge fight with his wife. Next thing I knew the blokes were asking me to tell them some of my story's about the drugs. I didn't really want to tell them anything but eventually I agreed "everyone turn there lights off" i said. That way we would see anybody approaching as it was instant dismissal for laying down underground so the boys did that and I told them a story. I had been working at north goonyella Colliery a couple of months prior with SBD Mining services. It was SBD services first longwall move and they really wanted and needed to do this job and do it right as doing it right would ensure they would get future contracts. The longwall is a giant continuous miner that might be 200metres in length. Length or width across the coal cutting face depending on how you look at it. It mines or extracts a 200 metre wide bite of coal and continues that for 2 or 3 kilometres. Its like a really wide front end loader bucket if it was 100 two metre wide pieces bolted together. There is a face conveyer chain that runs from side to side and the shearer or coal cutting tool cuts the coal as if the loader bucket had a saw blade zinging along the front of it. The coal then falls onto the conveyer which feeds it to one side and off to surface. The front end loader bucket is supported by hundreds of hydraulic rams round as 44 gallon drums. They hold up the roof and have ski pontoons that slide along the floor. Another hundred hydraulic rams are laying down pushing forward the loader bucket and the longwall machine keeps moving continuously. It all slides forward when pressure is released in the Rams. The rams then push upwards again supporting the roof from falling in. Its driven by electric cables and hydraulic pumps and thousands of hoses. Once it cuts out the 3 kilometre block the roof falls down behind it and you can't back up the machine. The machine is then pulled apart to move it somewhere else. SBD mining services had signed a contract saying they would pull apart this giant machine and move it. They also signed to put it back together again. They signed saying it would be done a certain way and in a certain time using a certain amount of men or manpower. All the men which they had agreed to provide had not turned up. at first they thought there company was going to breach the contract and they would be sued and they actually thought that was the end of SBD services as it would clearly ruin them but it wasn't the case. The bosses worked out that if the men that were there worked 12 hours a day and only 2 shifts instead of 3 it would be fine. Do that and they could meet the needs of the contract. We would do it but we had to do it with no days off. The contract would take about 9 weeks and the only time we got a break was the change over shift. This meant 6 days on one day off then 6 nights on one day off and so on. No one could go home as we were 5 to 6 hours drive away from Mackay and about 7 or 8 hours away from Rockhampton. If you drove home by the time you got there and slept you would have to drive straight back. Eventually we had worked ourselves ahead of schedule. It was right near the end of the contract so they decided to let everyone have 4 days off. Everyone except me and Dallas. Dallas and I were only allowed to have 3 days off. We had to stay and work. The SBD services owner wanted to buy me and Dallas a few drinks. Problem is when I drink I want to have drugs. I got half full of alcohol and started thinking about it. I started saying to the owners son "how long does it usually take to get to Mackay from here" and "is the airport easy to find" I asked him to show me on the map as there were no GPS navigation for drivers in those days. He asked where I was going and I said "its a 2 hour flight to Sydney Simon I'm going to have 48 hours fun and fly back". He tried to talk me out of it and it almost worked but once I had that thought in my mind the monkey on my back is very hard to shake. It's like not scratching a itch, it's impossible so away I went to Mackay. I flew to Sydney after a quick stop in Brisbane. In Sydney my best friend was John tanner. He's the one that lived in the house over grown with blackberry bushes. The house was his grandmother's before she died and on the property's were 2 Apple orchids. There was one either side of burragorang road. He lived there with his older brother Dale and the younger brother Noel. He was waiting on a compensation payout a rather large one from a car accident. My mate Dirt was driving and killed johns fiancée Dianne. We called Dirt Dirt as his brother was called clay. With Dirt driving they drove head-on into a rock wall on Christmas day about 5 years earlier. John wasn't a small guy he was rather big and his body weight whilst sitting in the back seat is what likely killed her. He didn't give a shit, he didn't even go to her funeral. He said they were fighting and that he'd had enough. They were in a 2 door HOLDEN LJ TORANA. Johns Mrs had a medical certificate saying she didn't have to wear a seatbelt and she demanded to sit in the front seat. If she had of just been gracious like most women she would have sat in the back after all she wasn't driving with John driving and in someone else's car. John sat behind her and because it was a 2 door the bucket seats have a little spring loaded catch. You flip the catch and the seat folds forward. They hit the rock wall head on at speed and John had not put a seatbelt on. His huge body weight went crashing through the seat breaking the catch. The weight of him smashed his Mrs even harder into dashboard killing her. John went through the seat so hard he snapped both his legs half way between his knees and his hips. The thema bone is the strongest bone in the human body and very hard to break. The bone was hit by impact on the ends of it. The impact hit end to end down the bone long ways and would be like a pool cue snapping from hitting a pool ball. It just doesn't happen. John's brother Noel was in the back also not wearing a seat belt. Noel was left with severe brain damage and had already received 1 million dollars compensation. He owned the two story house next door to johns. He bought it off his father because his mother and father had split. The father used to say the mother living across the road drove him crazy and he had to move away. It was like the my 3 son's or Mr Ed television show except they weren't living with the dad. There mother tried as hard as she could to keep me away from the brothers. I would lead them astray she would say but it was the other way around. All 3 were in the paper for one of the largest marijuana crops in NSW for that time. Dale aged 17 or 18 John aged 14 and Noel aged 11. They were bad to the core and leading me astray all the time. The older brother got the grandmother's cockatoo and hooked it up to 240 volts and turned the power on. He did that just to spite the grandmother because she wouldn't give him a cigarette. John now had a prostitute for a girlfriend called Angie and she was a good one. A absolute workaholic that didn't use drugs. She owned her own home and bought John expensive clothes, rolled gold earing's, diamond studs and Rado watches. I used to live with John, we both slept together in a king size bed. Of course I'm not poof but try to tell his Mrs that. When you are on the heroin you don't roll over in your sleep you just lay flat on your back. The nodd they call it. I feel I know Angie well as the phone was on my side of the bed and when she'd ring almost every night I would answer. John hadn't gone to see her for months maybe as many as 5. On heroin men don't want sex sex is that last thing blokes want and they say your in love with the pink lady. Sometimes pure heroin is a nice pink or a pale brown crystal rock that you rarely see it these days. Most of the stuff we get is white from cutting compounds. I called John on the phone to tell him I was coming. I needed him pick me up and knew he'd be there waiting as he would do anything for a shot of heroin. He didn't work he just lived in the overgrown house. The house only had floorboards in 3 rooms and use to get the odd funnel web spider. John and Noel were at the airport waiting. Noel had a brand new Holden Commodore he bought one every 2 years but even though he got his million dollars he was still broke. Because he had brain damage all the money was in trust for him and he only got enough to buy a house a car every second year and about $100 interest each day. He chain smoked most of the money and the rest would go in the poker machines. He had calices on the end of his fingers from whacking the buttons so hard. They both had no money. John hadn't seen his Mrs for 5 months and every cent he got went to support his heroin habit. It was good to see them I'd been away 8 weeks so I jumped straight in the car and John said "Cabramatta man or what" He couldn't believe the size of me he said. Incase it wasn't obvious Cabramatta is where the heroin is and it was ran by Asians. Cabramatta was a town built entirely for Asians. It was like China town but for Vietnamese and Cambodian migrant refugees. "Big rock make you lay down" the Asians said as we hit the streets. You don't really need to get out of the car they'll almost fight to get to serve you first. Some can't even speak English big wock (rock) with there accent is all you could understand. Some didn't speak at all they nodded at you a lot and i've got to give it to them they flooded the place with heroin. There were so many dealers the price of heroin was cheaper then marijuana. $25 a cap buy 3 and you got it for $60. If it's your first time a cap will kill you. You get 3 goes out of one cap of pure and people were dying all the time. Some were happy to. It ain t that bad it just depends how you go I suppose. Noel didn't use the heroin he didn't need to. Of a night time he would call out to his uncle John to get the shot gun saying he's going to kill a bloke name Smally or a lawyer named John Marsden. Yeah Noel talked to himself and didn't know it. He thought because we could hear his thoughts that the surgeons put microphones in his head. He thought they did it during the surgery after the accident. "I'm gonna blow ya fucking head off Marsden" he would yell out over and over and over again. John Marsden was his lawyer. He came up with a idea to trick Noel as a way to stop him thinking about the microphones in his head. Marsden told Noel "yes ok they put microphones in your head" "we will put you back in hospital and have them removed" and they actually staged it. They put Noel in hospital and made out they did brain surgery. The doctors even glued fake stitches and shaved a patch of hair. It didn't work because when he drives the car its just as bad. When Noel drives he snickers "siss siss siss siss siss" then yells out "he knows he knows ha ha ha ha ha and laughs his guts out. He then says in a really evil voice "drink it bitch every last drop" he does this all the time and of course his brother takes the piss out of him and says "who fucking knows ya stupid cunt" Noel knew it was all bullshit and the solicitor lied to him so every night he wants to kill the solicitor. Pretty dangerous while he was driving down the road "he knows he knows ha ha ha ha ha. Every now and then John would grab the wheel and say "look out Noel" and jerk the car back to the right side of the road. We drove to Bob Jane Tyre Mart at Campbelltown on blacksland road as they had the car booked in to get new tyres. John had forgotten I hadn't used heroin for 8 weeks my tolerance was back to zero he just talked while he mixed up the shot. We sat in the car while they changed the tyres. We didn't care we used to shoot up in the back of taxi cabs while we were driving along. He mixed up a shot and gave me half. I didn't feel a thing I just remember coming to "boof" it went as I went thru the rubber flaps at the hospital. I had overdosed and died multiple times and John kept reviving me. He would revive me while Noel drove.

Apparently when the hospital staff came to get me out of the car I kept trying to fight them off. John got a wheel chair and wheeled me thru the rubber doors. After I was discharged I came across a old friend from school Dave. Dave suggested going to the casino and I had never been so I agreed. John wasn't up for the casino neither was Noel so we were going to have to catch a train. I went and bought myself some new clothes. I bought a Swede jacket along with a new watch and away I went to the casino. Once at the casino Dave tried to show me around some of the smaller tables but it was very crowded. We went out front to a bar to have a couple of quiet drinks and talk. While talking Dave was escorted off the premises by bouncers. I'm not sure if he had done something in the past or perhaps he didn't meet the dress code I'm not sure but I was now on my own. I eventually made my way back in to the tables as I wanted to learn black jack. On the smaller $5 bet tables there is so many people it's very hard to sit and watch. I was walking around and I noticed a few tables off to the side. These tables to the side didn't seem to have many people at them. I approached a table with only one Asian guy playing. He had what would have been his wife with her hand on his shoulder watching. It was a high roller $50 minimum bet table that's why it wasn't crowded. Not many people can bet big bets. Most stick below $25 and most of the $50 high roller tables were empty. As I approached the table the Asian said "you play one bok" "you play one bok It's better" I didn't have a clue what he was talking about. I told him I didn't know how to play and he said again "you play one bok one bok is better put money here" he pointed tapping the table. I pulled a few hundred dollars out of my pocket and got the dealer to cash it in for chips. Again he says "you play one bok" "put money here" tapping the table. I eventually worked out one bok meant play one box and he wanted me to put my money behind his. "is better one bok trust put money here" he insisted so I did. On the table is a square box marked out. One box for every person sitting at the table. The box is yours, it's where your cards are placed so you can be separated and distinguished from anyone playing beside you. So I listened to the Asian and I put my money behind him and he won. He would tell me when to bet the money and also when not to and most of the time he was right. Most of the time he would win. He was clearly counting cards. In time I picked up on how to play. I wanted to open my own box and play for myself. Every time I tried to get the dealer to deal to me the Asian would say "no no no you play one bok one bok is betta "so I put my money back behind him. I must admit I was up a couple of thousand dollars playing this way but I was really wanting to have a go for myself. I had to do it I had to have a go and eventually I got the dealer to deal to me. The Asian was saying over and over "you play one bok one bok is betta "I lost a couple in a row but I kept wanting to play my own hand. The Asian was now cursing me in Asian I couldn't understand a word he was saying. Its hard to understand the Asians but I could tell he was angry. He left the table. It was clearly ruining his count because he started losing. Every time he would lose he would curse me "one bok you play one bok is betta" he was dirty at me and very angry. I had the game worked out a little bit and I was having fun. A new dealer had came on a female about 29 or 30 years old. The dealers change every hour. Two dealers deal on two tables and every hour they swap dealers. They do that and usually once per shift they swap out all the cards. She wasn't supposed to help me she said but she gave me a few pointers." Would you like a drink sir "she asked "scotch and lemonade "I replied, drinks were complimentary "here let me light that cigarette" she would say every time I had a smoke. She was great. There was nobody there except me and her. I was pretty sure no-one could hear us talk. She indicated it was against the rules for her to instruct me but she taught me how to split my hands. At times when you get a pair you can choose to separate the cards and have the dealer flip cards onto two individual hands. She pretty much showed me how to play. It wasn't long before I noticed I had a huge pile of chips 5 or 6 stacks of $100 chips 12 chips in every stack. I noticed she would say "more bets more bets" then pause and then say "more bets more bets "then wave her hand across the table and say "no more bets". After she said no more bets you couldn't put any more money down but before she said no more bets you could put more chips on the table. What she was doing was really simple. When it was going to be a winner she would say "more bets more bets "then pause then say again "more bets more bets "and I would put a heap more chips out and the hand would win. When it was going to lose she would simply say "more bets more bets, no more bets "straight away so I couldn't get another bet on. It took me hours to be sure that that's what she was doing. She would go on break and I would have 20 or 30 thousand maybe more on the table. People especially Asians would see all the money and think I was counting cards. They would come and put there money behind me. When they did this she would do the reverse. She would get me to put more money on the table by saying "more bets more bets "and pausing. When I put on more bets, so would the Asians. They would stack $4000 or more behind mine and she would take everyone's money. That way it kept her float of money up and it wouldn't appear she was giving a heap to me. Every time the dealer changed it would be the same young guy. He was really good. He would clean me out almost then she would come back on and build me up again. One time I had lost all of my money. I went and drew out the last $900 out of my bank account. The $900 was to buy a airfare to fly back to work in Mackay without it I had no money and no way of getting back to work. I lost that last $900 all the way down to $200 and she came back on shift and built me back up again. She eventually said to me "when I come back next time it's my last shift, you better be there with all that money because after that I'm going home and your coming with me "I didn't know What to think. I didn't know if she was going to take it all back before she went. I didn't know if she wanted to take half of the money and meet up some where to split it up. I didn't know What she meant. The other dealer had come back on shift and was making short work of the 40 thousand I would have had. I got nervous and pulled the pin and stopped playing. 11 thousand dollars I cashed in and left. I caught a cab the 1 hour and 20 minutes drive home. The whole way I felt I was being watched and I waited to be pulled over but it never happened. I had no part in it and still to this day am unsure if she was doing it intentionally. Perhaps I was just lucky I guess I'll never know. I was meant to catch a plane back to Mackay that morning. By the time I arrived at johns place I simply didn't have time to make it to the airport. I checked when the next available flight was and there was one about

4pm that afternoon but I missed that one as well. I rang work and told the secretary but she said she was sure it would be fine. She told me to catch the next available flight to Mackay and she said that they could swap the shifts I usually worked and put me on a different shift with a different crew of blokes. I booked and paid for the airfare. There was seven hours to kill before I could catch the next one. You couldn't smoke in the airport terminal to smoke you had to go outside where the taxis pulled up. I was standing there and next minute a taxi driver with a wog accent rolls down his window and says "are you right man" I replied "Yeah mate just waiting for the plane." I told him I had to wait seven hours to which he said "you need prostitute" but I wasn't really the type to get prostitutes. I had done it twice in my life, once when I was 17 years old and very drunk and once in Kalgoorlie western Australia. I said to him "where do we get prostitutes, up kings cross? also saying that I didn't find the girls in the brothels there much good. I said "they aren't real nice" he told me he knew of a better place where there were beautiful girls just on the side of the road "is it Canterbury road" I asked but he said "no, Darlinghurst". Darlinghurst wasn't far from the airport so I jumped into the taxi. I liked the way he talked and I had nothing better to do. We pulled into this road in the middle of the city, the street was on a hill sloping down and I had never been there before. He started pointing out all the women. They stood out as all they were wearing was underwear, high heels and fishnet stockings. He pulled over and started talking to them. He would say "yo baby how much" and ask them "do you do everything including French". French meant give oral sex. Most of the woman said "yes" and they all would say "No kissing on the lips". We would have a bit of chat with a girl and then move on to the next one and we did that several times. Next minute there was a really hot brunette chick. She was about 21. She was wearing a jumper and tight jeans and didn't look like a prostitute but he yelled out "hey come here baby girl" "what's your name" "Shelley" she said "your a worker yes?" he questioned her making sure she was. She was gorgeous and I told him what I thought as we chatted to her. She was easy to talk to and looked real clean and healthy. Some of the other girls looked a bit run down. She was just like a girl you would take home to meet your mother and I told him "yeah I like this one". He told her I had to wait seven hours for a plane and she said "six hours would be $450 "I said it was a deal as long as we could get a room away from that area. I didn't want a room that the pimp new of as he might rob me when I had my pants down. We drove over near central train station and got out at a hotel motel. I paid the taxi driver and Shelley and I walked in and booked a room. While walking up the stairs I asked her if she could score any good drugs and she said" is the pope a catholic" that meant yes. We put our bags in the room and headed up the road. I had flown all that way and only had one shot of heroin. We walked down the road past the entrance of Sydney's central train station and turned left up these deserted alley ways. There were no people and no cars and I realized I had ten thousand dollars on me. I started thinking I was going to be robbed. She walked me deeper into these alley ways further away from people and I became quite scared. She had seen the big roll of cash I had in my pocket when I got out $300 for the heroin. Next minute she said "wait here I'll be back in minute" My heart was in my throat but she was only around the corner for 20 seconds. On the way back she asked if we could go to a payphone as she needed to tell her boyfriend (pimp) how long she would be so he wouldnt get worried. Once back in the room I handed her the heroin and told her to take as much as she needed to inject. $300 worth of heroin was actually a lot and about ten shots for me so I told her to take what she needed. I explained I better mix up a shot to inject separate as my tolerance was low. I told her I'd been away working and had been off the heroin for 8 weeks. I felt really comfortable with her and we got along well. I wasn't lost for words like you sometimes get with some woman. She was hot and I told her that. Although men don't want sex when on heroin I couldn't help myself I had to have her so we had good sex then chatted for a while. She told me how she had only just started being a prostitute. She had come to Sydney to be a fashion designer but got with a guy that got her hooked on drugs. To my surprise she pleaded to come to Mackay with me. I wanted to take her but I had no place for her to stay while I was at work. Finally I made it back to the airport just in time to catch the plane. I ended up that off my face I struggled to drive the four and a half hours back out to north goonyella mine. Being on heroin made you feel very sleepy and it was like being in that slumber when you don't want anyone or anything to wake you up. You are almost dreaming while you are awake Next thing we heard a machine coming. I said to the men to stand up. I didn't want to get caught laying down as it's a sack able offence. We all put our cap lamps on and made it look as if we were doing something as the machine came around the corner but it was just one of our guys. The guys all said they liked the story's, everyone except Jim Leak. "A bit different to our weekends mowing the fucking lawn Demo" one bloke said another saying "wish I was bloody single I'd be coming with you". Jim Leak was angry with me because we didn't work that day. Later after the shift Jamie went to the owner of Mastermyne and accused me of injecting drugs in the car park. Lee Beckart the owner sacked me and I was out of a job. I wasn't happy. I was very comfortable working for Mastermyne. It was a long time since a company had supplied me with work clothes that had my name on them. I had worked hard to get to where I was and I felt part of a team. I liked everyone and everyone liked me. The men I worked with almost went on strike. Everyone was angry over it as Mastermyne didn't give me the opportunity to have a drug test. Working whilst under the influence was not something I did. Every mine site had drug testing and I had never failed one even though I used drugs on days off Sometimes. Dick Lock rang and said to have a independent drug test so I did and the drug test was negative. Lee Beckart offered me my job back approximately 3 days later but it was too late. When I was told I was sacked I rang Brent Gorome from ready work force and they had given me a much higher paying job and I couldn't turn the job down. I tried but they already signed a contract saying they were providing me as specialized labour at Glenden's Newlands Colliery. I was happy and I received extra pay to fill out everyone's time sheets and submit them every week. I got more money working for 4 days on 4 days off then I did working 6 days for Mastermyne. I was hired to a company called valley longwall international to attempt to break a world record drilling. It was Diamond drilling basically except horizontal instead of vertically. The drilling rig was Brand new and we had brand new technology that would enable us to steer the drill rods called the Mecca. It was great as no one new it's potential or how deep we could drill. At that time the current world record length or depth was around 900 metres. The reason that was as far as anyone had drilled before is because your drilling horizontally. Drilling horizontal holes made it very hard to steer the direction of the hole which I'll explain. You are not drilling downwards you are drilling straight out in front of you into the coal. The coal seam is like the layer of cream in a sponge cake except it's hard and the sponge cake above and below is made of rock. So imagine a giant sponge cake made of rock on top and rock on bottom and the cream layer is coal. Imagine drilling through the coal layer and out the other side without touching or running into any rock. As you extend the drill rods outwards they flex and bend like a fishing rod. The downwards weight causes the drill to drill down eventually running into rock. Valley longwall anticipated drilling much further then 900 metres. Prior to the Mecca being developed the only way to steer or know where the end of drill was, was by sending a camera down the inside of the drill rods and taking a photo. There would be a compass in front of the camera that showed North south east and west along with longitude and latitude and height above sea level. Once that photo was taken you developed the photo and plot your course on grid paper. It was not easy at all and was very time consuming. It was exciting times and a great bunch of guys. I only worked with 2 others on my shift, Jay fisher and the driller. One night while loading drill rods to take under ground the owners son came to talk to us he said "hi fellas working hard I see "we replied "yes" then to my surprise he asked "Jay is it true your wife is a undercover cop" Jay answered "yes but it's suppose to be a secret" "how cool does she catch serial killers" the owners son was saying. Jay shut him down stating he wasn't allowed to talk about it. I don't like cops but did think it was cool as I would be able to probe him later with questions. Jay fisher was new to underground mining. He had first went underground about 7 months prior at central Colliery. He worked for VLI and was a trainee driller. At central VLI employees were not allowed to operate any machinery and most of them had no authorizations. The driller and shift boss was this old guy and he drove me and Jay nuts. He kept teaching Jay wrong things and would stop drilling to go outside for a smoke. We were trying to break a world record and shift records to go with it. He was breaking all the rules and endangering our lives and lives of every man underground. In the coal we were drilling into is pockets of the gas methane. These pockets have massive amounts of pressure and you have to drill ahead before you mine to release that pressure otherwise when the men start tunnelling the pressure causes the coal to blow out and buries everyone. Drilling ahead allows us to bleed off the pressure. Whilst we were drilling we hit a massive pocket of methane. The pipes used to bleed the gas off had busted somehow and methane was filling up the area Where we were working. The personal gas alarms we were wearing went off as breathing in the gas will kill you. Instead of evacuating the boss ignored the gas alarms and ordered Jay stay there and keep working. He tried to do the same with me. Jay didn't know right from wrong and was scared of losing his job if he didn't do as he was told. I shut the valve and evacuated immediately and told them both to do the same. The shift boss wouldn't listen and continued working which was highly illegal as methane in large quantities will spontaneously combust. Spontaneously combust means explode and kill us and the other 50 men working in the mine. I grabbed Jay and went outside and wrote a report about what had happened and within a couple hours the shift boss had his marching orders and was sacked. Jay was now the boss on that shift as there was no one else. The previous guy was told leave town immediately as the town was owned by the mining company. Jay and I would become very close as a result of that and he opened up to me about his wife. She worked in the east coast tactical drug squad as a undercover police officer. At the time she was posing as a iron man triathlete racing surf life saving boats. Police had 2 teams of men and woman as they had a sporting star under surveillance. VLI brought in Frank Russell to continue Jason's training so we could keep drilling. We managed to break the shift record and passed the current world record easily. The new Mecca gave us a real time computer display of exactly where the end of the drill was at all times. Usually steering the end of the rods at the depth of a thousand metres was impossible. They call the drill rods a string line of rods because it bends like a string. The longer the string line the more it bends. We drilled with such accuracy we ended up stopping at 1850 metres. We pulled back to half way and branched off our original hole and at 1400 metres we steered the rods back into the hole. We could of kept on drilling but we had proven the Mecca was a success. Prior to the development of the Mecca the only way to steer the rods is via a down hole motor and taking a photo as I said earlier. The drills rods don't spin only the cutting bit on the end of the rods spins. This is achieved by a down hole motor. A down hole motor is a lot of gears like in a gear box. The cog mechanism that turns the gears is turned by water pressure. The down hole motor is a approximately a 4 metre section as round as the rods and it contains gears. On the very end or tip of the down hole motor is the cutting head or bit, and its diamond toothed. Water pressure is pumped down the entire inside of the rods and turns the gears which turn the cutting head. The cutting head sits slightly offset of centre causing it to steer to one side. you put the offset at 9am to the left side and drill for 4 rods. That causes it to steer left of Centre. The rods are 3 metres in length and screw together. Then you turn all the rods clockwise until the offset is at 3pm and drill for 4 rods. The cutting tip will steer the drill back past centre and off to the right. You then turn the offset back to 9 am again and drill another 4 rods and so on. The hole zig zags left and right all the way, It doesn't go straight at all. With the Mecca it was more like having a video camera down the cutting end of the drill at all times. The Mecca fed a image straight into a computer monitor displaying exactly the time the offset was drilling at and it's coordinates Height above sea level and longitude latitude and it displayed it in a series of different graphs and maps. To steer upwards you mark the rods with a chalk mark representing the offset motor at 9am. You then fasten a big multi grip wrench or stilzens and turn the chalk mark to 12 o'clock. It was often necessary to drill up because the weight of the rods caused it to drill down into the rock floor. Before the Mecca the only way of knowing you were in the rock floor was the colour of the water that returns. The water flows inside your drill rods turning the gears and through the middle of the cutting head or bit. The water then returns outside the rods flushing out the grit from cutting through the coal. If the water turned white you would know it was in Rock. The Mecca gave us a real time display and we could see when it was starting to steer towards the floor. We would then drill upwards and bring it back to centre. We also saved all the time sending down cameras. We broke the shift records and the world record by double. No one knows exactly how far the Mecca could drill. It was a simple innovation as all they did was put battery terminals on either end of each 3 metre length of rod. Then wires running down the middle connected the battery terminals on both ends. When the drill rods screw together the battery terminals touch and connect the wires. The end result is a live feed to a monitor display of exactly where the rods were at all times. I'm not sure if that record has been broken today. It would be possible to drill as far as the drill rig is capable of pushing, remembering the further you go outwards the heavier the drill rods are to push. As it is the drill rig is chained and bolted down with 4 ft steel bolts into solid rock. This is to stop it from sliding back as you push the drills into the coal.

CHAPTER 7

One White Shoe, One Black Shoe

I was back in Rockhampton in a motel with Sheridan. We had planned to score drugs from calliope a town 100 kilometres away. Because I was running low on money Sheridan had said she would sell some drugs to get my money back. Sheridan mixed up a shot for both of us to inject. I was always concerned when someone mixed up a shot for me as people get killed that way. I watched carefully to make sure I knew exactly what I was injecting. I remember questioning her "isn't it a bit big for the two of us" "narr" she said "it will be right". She told me a good fry shot makes tinkbelle come out and she laughed. I watched as she shot up what was supposed to be half. She coughed n gagged a bit "woo fuck yeah "she said as the beads of sweat started to pour down her forehead. She encouraged me to have mine saying "go on it's your turn". I injected half and stopped pushing the plunger on the syringe. I paused while the needle was still in my vein. I did this stopping half way when injecting heroin so I could tell if I was injecting to much. "I might only have the half "I said knowing the full shot was going to be too much. "you'll be right "she said saying she did it and was fine. I pushed the remaining half into my vein. I knew straight away I had had to much. The rush just kept climbing and there was a white pinging noise between my ears. The pinging noise was the same as the old Tv's used to make when the tv station was shut down. The tv would display a pattern and a high pitched frequency or squealing noise could be heard. My head pinged and squealed like that and I gagged a little like I was going to vomit "I've had to much" I complained but she laughed at me so I had no choice but to try and laugh back. I was in a daze I couldn't focus and I was starting to feel a little scared. I had done this to myself plenty of times but only when I was on my own. Being that dazed left you incapable of defending yourself. When I was alone in a motel it was ok as there wasn't anyone there to cause me harm. Sometimes I would pass out and would wake up hours later on the bed. Being with someone you don't know or trust that well was scary. I didn't let on as I didn't want Sheridan to know how fucked up I was. She toyed with me while we were driving "ready to play tinkerbells Game "she kept saying over and over and laughing. I couldn't talk all I could do was laugh a little. She drove straight past Rockhampton and to Mackay. She drove out in the cane fields where no one knew where I was. It was scary as I was 300 kilometres away from where I was meant to be. The last point of contact was the motel I had checked out of and the ATM machine I used. Friends and family thought I would have already left for Sydney, and that was the opposite direction. Could she be doing this deliberately I was thinking. Who were all these strange people she was introducing me to I thought. We were at a house owned by Carol but we didn't stay long. She took me to a motel that had two males and a female inside. Sheridan explained that one of the guys we were going to meet was Tooney a local underworld figure and well known meth cook. The other guy was named Eimeo. I couldn't really talk so I just sat quite and listened and played the tight lipped sort of bloke. That was all I could do as my brain was fried. I couldn't really join into any of the conversation I just laughed every now and then. Eventually Sheridan said she had to take Tooney and his girlfriend somewhere. She said for me to wait there with Eimeo. "I'll be back soon "She said and she blew me a kiss. It wasn't long before I realized Eimeo was suffering psychosis. He kept looking out the windows holding the curtains back and saying "I see you out there you can't hide from me". He had a army knife in his hand and he kept asking me who I was and how did I know Sheridan and Tooney etc. I was freaking out as guys in this state will kill you if you give the wrong answer. Now he was holding the door open as well yelling to someone who wasn't there. Next minute his phone rings and he answers "hello!, yes he's here why" then hands me the phone. It was Tooney "sorry" he said. He had come to realize the state Eimeo was in and admitted they probably shouldn't have left me with him. He asked "what's he like now" indicating to not let him know I was talking about him. "What are they saying" Eimeo started asking whilst looking out the curtains. "what the fuck do they want and what's with all this secrecy" Eimeo said as he grabbed the phone. He argued for a minute and then hung up. He was straight back to the front door and had it wide open. He was cursing someone and saying to me "there fucked I'm gonna stab the motherfuckers" Just then I had a lightbulb moment. Im not sure what made me think of it but I'm glad I did. I said I would go and sort it out and slipped out the door and off I went. I walked to the front of the motel and as soon as I got passed the main office Sheridan pulled up in my car and said "get in" she apologized and drove about 3 kilometres back into the Cane fields to carols place. As soon as we pulled up a undercover police car pulled up behind us. They told us both to get out of the car. A female was asking Sheridan for her license, while the male cop asked for my identification. He was looking through my wallet "coal miner huh?" he said before questioning me why I had no license. "good thing your not driving" he said with a stern voice before pulling out my VLI identity card. "hey isn't this who ya husband works for" he said to his partner. She shrugged her shoulders and said "no" and put her finger to her lip making a gesture that it was a secret. "It's who your husband works for he said again "telling her to come and have a look. She came around to my side of the car and looked. She said she was really sorry to me and I knew straight away it was Jay's wife. The male officer said he wanted to search me. He asked Carol if there was a room and she pointed to the bathroom "Yeah just go in there" she said. The cop took me in the bathroom and frisked me with a hand search. He made me spread my arms and legs and lean against the wall. He kept talking while patting me down "where's all the pink champagne "he asked. I didn't know they called speed or amphetamines pink champagne. I had never heard of it before and didn't know what he was talking about. "am I supposed to bring some chicken" I joked "wise guy huh" he said. I told him I had no idea what he was talking about. "Im from Sydney" I said. He replied "the speed I'm talking about speed". Carol and her friends were in the room next door. The walls were only thin and I knew they could hear everything so I told him nothing I just stuck to my story that I didn't know what he was talking about. He eventually let me put my pants and shirt back on and they left. A couple hours later carols man walked in and said he had to shake my hand. I asked what for "I haven't done anything". He told me he was on the run and the cops came looking for him. He said I distracted them and he ran away into the Cane fields and that they came almost every second day. Carol told everyone what she had heard through the walls "tight lipped this one" she said "he didn't say anything". It didn't matter the suspicion that I was a undercover cop was still there. They all heard the female cop apologize to me so they still had suspicion on there minds. That was early hours of the morning and the sun was just coming up when the cops left. Later that day we were driving into town to give someone a lift to the bottle shop. We saw the same un-marked police car and they waved to us from the opposite set of lights. Over the next few days I was left at the house. Sheridan kept taking off in my car for long periods at a time. I didn't have a clue what she was doing but now I would say she was doing sudi runs. Pseudoephedrine or sudi is in cold and flu tablets most commonly named Sudafed. Tooney was a meth cook they said but I didn't have any idea what he was doing. It seemed all the meth or speed came from Tooney and some of it he made. Whilst Sheridan was gone there was this chick named Coralline. She was a pretty scattered sort of chick. She made me take my clothes off so she could wash them and she gave me clothes that were from her dead husband who was found hanging in suspicious circumstances. The clothes were out dated and weird and I didn't like wearing them. The fact they were taking my clothes and washing them made me think they were getting any forensic evidence off them whilst dressing me in someone else's clothes was partially concealing my identity. On any surveillance video I would be wearing different clothing to the clothing last seen by video surveillance in Rockhampton. This made me Very frightened of what they might do. They kept entertaining almost every criminal in town and it was like they were all coming there to meet me some would even say they had heard about me. They would all ask me did I like fishing. Fisher was the last name of the female officer that apologized. I didn't know if it was a coincidence or not. They all bragged about they're crimes. One guy telling me how he put a huge safe in the back of a little two door hatch and it was hanging out the back making the car do wheel stands up the road. I didn't want to know. Knowing means when they get busted they think because you knew you dobbed them in. Its there own loose lips getting them busted by telling everyone. Everyone knows the saying "loose lips sink ships" My dad always said "birds of a feather all flock together "and to not hang with the people known to be bad birds. It makes you look bad and you'll be blamed for things they do. It's true criminals always flock together or associate with other criminals. Police can easily see who's in cahoots with who. I was scared of them taking my clothes and making me look like someone else. They drove me to another bottle shop in a car that was probably stolen. Coralline made me get out of the car and walk around so I was on video surveillance. Later that night Sheridan came and picked us up. She drove Coralline and me to a house in the middle of nowhere. It was dark so I had no idea of where I was. The house was occupied by one rather stocky criminal looking fella. I was brain fried still so I had no conversation with this man except answering a couple of questions. He said similar things to the others. He said he had heard of me and my blue Hyundai excel with the New South Wales number plates. The number plates stood out he said as we were in the state of Queensland. Half a hour later Sheridan vanished without telling me or Coralline. Coralline was scattered off her face and was under the house. She was going through buckets of nuts and bolts sorting them and talking in riddles. I couldn't make sense out of what she was saying. Alarmed I returned upstairs towards the room the guy was in and I heard him talking, it was obvious he was on the phone. I heard him say my name saying "narr that's him" I've got him here and he's all alone "he then repeated it by saying "yes he's by himself "I turned and walked straight back down the stairs. I physically grabbed Coralline underneath her arm Pitt and said "we've got to go". "Is Sheridan coming to pick us up" she asked so I just agreed. Making her think Sheridan is coming got her walking. "she's meeting us down the road" I told her. It was pitch black dark and I didn't have a clue where I was going. There were no lights and I couldn't see any in the distance I just walked as fast as could. We travelled about a kilometre and I kept bullshitting Coralline all the way. I kept saying Sheridan was coming and she'd meet us down the end of the road. Eventually in the distance I could make out a set of lights. "it's the service station" Coralline said. Now I new I was near safety I started interrogating Coralline "I accused her of setting me up and She eventually confessed. "it was Sheridan" "it was her "she said. We walked into the service station and I went to the pay phone. I pretended to ring a bloke I worked with named Mick. I made a fake call all about Sheridan and the people I was with. I spoke of the things that they had subjected me to and I said id see him soon. Coralline listened to the whole conversation and was completely fooled. I then rang my brothers answering machine and talked to it the same way. I was really angry and saying "I'll sort this Sheridan bitch out and tidy up the loose ends". Coralline started apologizing and trying to explain "they think your a cop "she was saying "it wasn't my idea "she pleaded. Then to my disbelief Sheridan drove in the driveway. She pulled up right out front of where I was standing. Furious I yanked the door open and ripped her out of the car. I yelled at her hard and threatened her. I told her "get in the back bitch" she was crying and saying sorry. I kept yelling as I drove away and she begged for forgiveness. Coralline started saying "it was all you bitch" "you deserve what's gonna happen to ya" it scared the hell out of Sheridan. But she eventually told me she went to find Tooney to swap the drugs for the car. Tooney was wanting to swap a ounce of pure speed and a small amount of cash for my car. This is why we went to that blokes house Sheridan said. The last thing I heard him say on the phone was "I don't know if he's already holding onto it "it was now starting to look like the guy new about the swap and was planning to rob me. I settled down and asked Sheridan if the swap was happening "yes I came looking for you to meet them" she said. I made Sheridan give me directions while I drove. She directed me to a bloke I hadn't met before. The bloke jumped into my car and introduced himself. He said he had to stop up the road and grab some things. I drove a couple of blocks and he told me to pull over at some shops and he ran down between them. He grabbed 2 round cardboard cylinders about 3 feet in length and jumped back in the car. There was a really strong smell of meth amphetamines, it smelled pretty strong. He yawned "arrrrgh" with his hand over his mouth "time for bed "he said "I'll get you to drop me home". Sheridan piped up all jovial "it's too late now, you had your chance but blew it" she said like she was saying it to spite me. I yelled at her some more until she started crying again. Then when I dropped the fella home and apologized. He said "narr that's fine by me id be pissed off to if I was you" he obviously knew the shit I'd been through and he obviously new Sheridan. We drove back to the service station. Sheridan received a phone call and it was Tooney and he wanted to meet up. He pulled in around the side of the service station. As I was walking from my car to Tooneys car a guy Sheridan said was wisey whistled me over. He said he had a heap of ecstasy tablets if I wanted to do a swap. "Be careful" he said opening up his jacket and pointing to a pair of headphones. "They'll be listening". I jumped in the back seat of Tooneys Holden Commodore "how ya going" he said "sorry for leaving you with Eimeo". Eimeo had got arrested not long after I left and was still in custody. Not much was known about that Tooney told me saying "your in the clear thus far" indicating they thought I might be involved in his arrest. All he had at that moment for the car was a quarter of a ounce. He went on to say if I could stay there until morning he would have the rest. He told me I could spend the night at his place and that it was with his parents. I had had enough of strange houses and I was fed up with these people. I was fed up with them thinking I was a dog or a cop and now they blamed me because Eimeo got busted. They are loose cannons and have themselves to blame. I told Tooney that I was going home that night and leaving very soon. He said he would give me the quarter of a ounce as a down payment and I could bring the car back or he could come down with me. He tried one last time to get me to stay. He tried bribing me saying he would drive down to Rockhampton with ounces and stay a few days. Then he said he would stay for good depending on how much stuff he could move. Again I refused. He picked his mobile phone up and said "he's on the moon "I'm not sure what he meant by that but it's how I remember his name. I just think of moon and Toon comes into my head. By the time we had got half way back to Rockhampton Sheridan was back into my good books. She had convinced me to pull over and have a sample of the Quarter ounce. She fried my brain once more and Corallines as well. "snap crackle and pop" she said. She was now driving and had all my drugs. She made me paranoid of police saying she would safe it if police came. Safing it meant to put it in her pussy. She kept saying I would go to jail if I got caught with that much and it was becoming clear why they called her Tinkerbelle. It was because she never comes when you want her to. Just like the cartoon she just turns up when she does. Back In Rockhampton I had to get away from her. She was taking me all over the place and introducing me to every criminal on the planet. She would have me red hot with police in 5 minutes and these crims would call cops just to see if I was a cop myself. That was the mentality of it. I left her and went to my brothers next door neighbours as I had no choice but to let Sheridan drive off with my car. When I would try to take the keys she would scream at the top of her voice "I've been selling drugs for you for weeks you bastard "she would scream out. I had no choice it was either have her scream until police turned up or let her go. Sheridan went with my drugs and a car that was part owned by someone else. Weeks went by and I hardly saw her. Without my knowledge she organized to sell my car to someone else I was just lucky he sought me out. Sheridan tried to get him to scam me for the rego papers. She wanted him to help trick me into signing the papers over but he was honest and didn't agree in ripping me off. Me and Scotty Bonelan had became buddys and needed somewhere to stay. Both of us were broke but the guy wanting to buy the car ran the biggest hostel in Rockhampton plus he sold drugs. He gave us half a ounce of rebels powder as a down payment on the car. It was shit stuff compared to pure meth and you needed to use a 8 ball between 2 people. He agreed to give us a room as well plus a ounce of pure when he could. He wanted us to sell drugs through him and deal it straight out of the hostel. I was in the phone box up the road telling Tooney what I had done. I needed to find out how much I owed him. Before I knew it Sheridan came running down the road wielding a claw hammer. "I'll kill you you fucking bastard "she said as she ran up to me "arrrgh arrgh arrrgh "she grunted swinging the hammer at my head. I was lucky I heard her coming or I would have copped it from behind "you fucking maggot" she said as she threw the hammer at me hitting me in the leg. I hadn't done her any wrong and I was in absolute shock as it was the other way around. I began a long campaign and started standing up for myself. I hated Sheridan and I never saw her again for years. Like anything in time you grew to appreciate it for what it was. She taught me a lesson in life and I wouldn't be the same person without it.

CHAPTER 8

Oztel Hostel

Scotty Boneland was about 26 years old and around 5.ft 8 inches tall. He had a heavily tattooed stocky build with short brown or black hair. He had lots of gold rings he inherited from his dead father as his father lived out the gem fields and mined sapphires. Scotty's rings rivalled uncle Norman's and they were quite nice to look at. He was a likeable character most of the time and he seemed genuine and loyal. That was comforting after the ride I had with Sheridan. We hit it off as he knew no one as well, at least that's what he told me and we both had no place to go. Two peas in a pod so to speak. It was stronger if there was two of us so we made a pact to stick together and to share our stuff equally. At Oztel hostel we were the guest of security guard and assistant manager Bernadus or Bernie we called him. Bernie was huge at least 6 ft 5 inches tall and really heavy set in his build. He had a big bikie beard and carried a half sized baseball bat like a club. It wasn't long and we had our ounce of pure. I sold the car to a car dealer to get $5000. I then gave the money to Bernie who then bought me a ounce of pure. A ounce probably sold for around 3500 dollars but expect to pay $4000 if you are using a middle man. We owed Bernie for half a ounce of powder and all the meals and accommodation he had provided the two of us. It had been about ten days since we first set foot in the place. We got straight down to business it was double your money with amphetamines. If you bought it for $4000 a ounce you could make $8000 back easy and do it in a day if done right. Most dealers in Rockhampton or anywhere don't put it out as pure they cut it. I wanted to leave it as close to pure as I could to take the business over quick. I made deals up and put them in water balloons just like the Asians in Cabramatta did. I carried the drugs in my mouth with a drink in my hand so I could swallow it should police come. I was expecting the police as people get dirty when you take over there business. I had all the intentions of being uncle Norman's and Roy Trifford's major competitors and to take them over. Because of there involvement with Sheridan I saw them as the enemy. It worked. I had the business in a few days and we were buying another ounce or 2. We had all the food, alcohol and fun we could cram in. Everything was perfect the only things we were missing was the girls. To me that hostel was dirty and wasn't the place to be courting girls but they came anyway. Johanna Martini was introduced to me by a woman I met named Rachel. Rachel had a husband and five kids. You couldn't tell she had kids at all as she had a nice figure. She was good-looking and never told me about her husband Glen. I never knew he existed until he rang my phone one day. Lucky he did ring otherwise I would have accidentally had sex with his wife. Life was good, we were dealing out of the biggest hostel in town. It was a bit of a dump but It had almost 60 rooms. Most of the customers lived at the hostel or in the surrounding neighbourhoods. Some lived at the saint Vincent DE Paul homeless shelter for men. Everyone would spend all they're money on drugs each week but you didn't need to buy food you could eat at the shelter as it had a soup kitchen and served 4 meals a day. In that environment everyone was broke and looking for a quick buck. If they were tough enough they would try and take my drugs. I only let a few know I had it and let them deal with all the people. The owners of the hostel seemed they were on our side. They had our back with police as well. Bill the hostel owner had regular contact with them when throwing people out. The owner bill had also nominated myself and Scotty as Mason lodge members. The dollar signs were starting to ring in my mind. Bill the owner didn't know we were selling drugs as he was drunk most of the time. He didn't know anything except how to have a good time. I recall at first he thought me and Scotty were there to do a hit on him. He thought the hit was for something he had done in his past. He also worried about his ex wives as he was a very wealthy man. I guess you have to be to own a 60 room hostel. We spent most of our time drinking with Bill, Bill and every publican on the south side of Rockhampton. There are a lot of pubs in Rockhampton, 52 at one stage but that included the surrounding areas. Because there was so much competition some looked to other things to make money and stay afloat. You don't have to do drugs to make money illegally especially When you have a pub or mason's lodge. Other things are easy to Organise if you have the capital. I also had a friend that worked for the main roads and transport department. This friend had sorted me a driver's license but I had given my identification to Scotty. He was to catch a bus as me and take drugs out west and start the business flowing into other towns. Instead of catching the bus Scotty lied and stayed in town and back doored me to uncle Norman. Turns out Scotty had a sister and she had kids to uncle Normans mate Roy. With the identification they obtained a driver's license and a motorcycle license. They borrowed money from finance companies and bought a brand new motorcycle a Yamaha R1. I never knew this until years later when state debt recovery contacted me. They contacted me about fines which I proved I was in another state at the time of the offence. I simply dug up my Centrelink records in another state and showed it couldn't have been me. When Scotty came back he came back empty handed so I took all his gold rings. The rings weighed a heap and had $1000 sapphires or aquamarine stones in them. Each ring would cost around $3000 in todays money and there were 4 of them. He had spent the week with a ex Mrs and Son and had used all the drugs. Roy and uncle Norman had corrupted him trying to get my contacts. That wasn't that easy. They couldn't just walk in with no money and trick credit out of these people like they usually did. There was no credit as it came from bikies as far as I knew, bikies that didn't give a fuck. The people didn't like junkies, they liked that I drank beer and tried to mix it with the men a little bit. I was new to the game but was learning fast. Scotty was out and it hurt me. I liked him and had invested a lot of hours bonding with him. he had a chopper reed look and way about him that balanced out my personality. Once a liar always a liar so he was no good to me anymore. He had caused me to get into a knife fight with Bernie my other partner in crime who also found it hard to only spend the profit. The best way to only spend the profit is to make the money back first. You don't spend anything the first day as it's not real hard to wait 24 hours. Then the next day you have the profit from the day before and you spend that keeping a day ahead of yourself. People seem to want to sell heaps of little deals thinking they make more. The more people you see the more it costs and the longer it takes. It also makes you red hot with police as too many know. It's best to sell bigger deals to other people who sell the little ones and let them see all the people. I had half a ounce left and Joanna with me. I decided I had had enough of the drug game and it was time to go to Sydney as I could sense danger all around me Because of the knife fight I had with Bernie. Billy the owner of the hostel was kicking us out anyway so I went and got Joanna and I a motel room. I decided we needed a day or two off the drugs as I didn't want me or someone else killed. Joanna had already done things to make me think she was a little crazy. When ever police would drive past she would start accusing me of calling them on her. when they'd drive past she would say "you dog cunt you called them on me didn't you "she had done this a few times and had not given me a straight answer about it. I wondered what was going on. She had just gone and done it again as police drove past she started saying "they told me you were a cop" she carried on as the police drove past thinking they were for her but of course they kept on driving. I said "not this time Joanna, this time your telling me what the fuck your talking about". At first she made out she didn't know what I was on about. I persisted with questioning her and she eventually told me she had shoplifting charges and she failed to appear in court for them. Her career criminal ex boyfriend was lieing to her. Her boyfriend Paul was in jail and had told her that fail to appear was very serious. He told her that when police caught up with her she would definitely go to prison. I told her fail to appear is very serious but because it's only shoplifting she would be fine. She could go get police to arrest her and charge her for fail to appear then plead guilty to the lot and she would only get a fine. She didn't trust me and wouldnt do that so I told her to stop spinning out and thinking I was a cop. I had had enough of her thinking I was setting her up with the detectives. She said she was also worried about being charged with my drugs as well so I went and got another motel room. One for the drugs and one for us. Whilst we relaxed in the motel room I made a lengthy phone call to John and Noel the brothers from Sydney. It was good to talk and all the bad feelings were disappearing. I could see a light appearing at the end of the tunnel and decided I was definately going to Sydney. Joanna was going to meet the ex boyfriend Paul and she had to be there the day he got out of prison as I had promised him that she would be. "great idea" she said asking "could we go for coffee "I agreed "coffee is a great idea let's go" I said. Rockhampton's main service station, truck stop and bus depot was straight across the road. We went and ordered coffees and a toasted sandwich and sat down whilst they made them. Two police officers working night shift on there lunch break walk in and say "hi how's your day been sir" "not to bad" I replied. Joanna started saying "don't talk to the scum" then she started "are you one of them" she was accusing me "fuck I'm fucked" she said as she folded her face into her hands to cry. I quickly grabbed her shoulder and stood her up saying" yeah a cigarette is a great idea, lets go" making out she was my girlfriend so I could man handle her. I dragged her outside and out of sight of the police. I explained "if I was a cop why would I drag it out, I would just arrest you". I told her if the police were here to arrest her they wouldn't order food they'd just arrest her and I calmed her down. We had a quick smoke and I encouraged her to come back inside. After grabbing the toasted sandwich and coffee we sat down. The police officers left and I spoke nice a calmly with Joanna. She was now laughing about it but just when I thought everything was fine two more police officers walked in. This time there was no stopping her. She got straight up and almost ran to the door. "gee is she ok mate" police said. I made out she was sick and just needed some fresh air. I went outside to try calm her down but the closer I got to her the worse she became so I stayed right away from her so she wouldnt start again. If that wasn't enough Roy Trifford and his brother were in a white Datsun 180 b and they came driving into the service station to get petrol. She went straight to them and started talking. Next thing I see is her leaving in the car with my enemies. I was furious she was drawing serious attention to me. All it would take is for the cops to actually watch for a second. If one started asking questions about the girl taking off I would be fucked. The guys she got in the car with were known drug dealers. The brother and guy in the back had been to prison and the one in the back was a known killer. Gunny was known for killing a young guy in prison but he hadn't been caught yet. I immediately realized I was outnumbered and couldn't go to there house. Feeling helpless but knowing I could straighten the shit out with police I went to talk to them. I told the desk sergeant about Joanna's problem. I told him it was just shoplifting and that she kept freaking out when we saw police. I asked him did he think I could get it fixed at court saying I was a coal miner. "let me check on the computer" he said asking what her name was. After he typed in her name he told me I could definately get it fixed "nothing serious" "where is she" he asked. I knew the house but didn't know the address. I didn't even know the street. He said "go and find it and when you do ring us and we will come and get her". I caught a taxi and eventually found the place but it took me hours as I kept going down the wrong street. Once I found the house I walked to the phone box up the end of the road and I rang the number on the card he gave me. The same sergeant answered. He told me to wait there saying officers would pick me up as again I didn't get the house number. About 15 minutes after a police car pulled up and started questioning me. I told them again that I didn't know the number and they told me to jump in the car to show them so I did. They pulled up out front and went and knocked at the door "is Joanna here "they said when the door opened. "yes I'll just go and get her" the person said giving her up straight away. The police tried to put her in the back with me and she kicked and screamed that much they made me get out. They put her in the back then radioed another car for me. Back at the station police informed me that she was wanted for very serious charges. They couldn't tell me exactly what they were they said and they told me to go home and have a sleep. The sergeant said to see him at 10am in the morning and he would tell me what to do. I went back to the motel feeling like a police informant and I felt pretty bad. I felt tricked by the police but if Joanna had of told me the truth it wouldnt have happened. If I had of known it was more then shoplifting I wouldn't of said a thing. In the morning I went and seen the desk sergeant it was the same one. He told me I could probably get her out if I listened and did what he said. "You go see a solicitor called Doug Winters" he said and he told me where to find him. When I saw Doug he told me it was going to cost me $5000 and I couldn't believe it it was only the year 2002. That's the equivalent to about 15,000 in today's money. He told me it was for outstanding fines but she didn't have any outstanding fines as her court matters had not been finalized. I asked for a receipt and he said "what for "and told me to listen and just trust him and he guaranteed he would get Joanna freed. I really wanted a receipt but I had no choice but to trust him. He made me stay outside the courts registry while he went in and pretended to pay the fines. He told me to go home and to meet at his office at 4pm. 4pm came and I went to Doug Winters office and met with him. We walked down to the court house and he disappeared down stairs into the police watchouse and holding cells to see Joanna. Court had closed for the day and by the time he re-appeared it was after 5 pm. He said to me "magistrate Henshaw is going to deal with it now just wait outside the court" but as soon as he walked into the courtroom I followed. "your honour I have the matter of Joanna Martini "he said. Henshaw replied "yes this is the matter in which the boyfriend is the actual perpetrator leaving the young lady to take the fall, is that correct "he said. Doug Winters went on to say "all outstanding fines have been paid as we agreed upon your honour "and he said that the $5000 was from a coal miner the new boyfriend of Ms Martini. He then looked around and said he is in court today your honour. The magistrate acknowledged me and released Joanna of all charges on the condition she resided with me. He wiped her record which left me wondering who I actually paid. It does make sense if the judge was being paid that he took smaller amounts opposed to large amounts as the small amounts would go un noticed. Anything above $10,000 deposited in a bank account these days is investigated by police. It may have only been $5000 but like I said it was only 2002. Say they went halves and the judge did that on average 3 times a week that $22,500 per month which is a quarter of a million each year. Joanna didn't have to face court again all she had to do was be picked up from custody by me. I went and waited around the back of the courthouse where they let people out of police custody. I had to wait about 20 minutes. Joanna was eventually released into my custody and off we went back to our motel room. Joanna was over whelmed by her ordeal and in disbelief of what had just happened. She had convinced me to let her go to Glenn and Rachel's place and she rang Racheal on the phone in the room. Racheal agreed to have her and came and picked her up. Racheal lived close to Roy Trifford's house the place where I had just arrested her from. I joked about not going there as she was leaving. Joanna hated cops and police informants with a passion. I was not a police informant that was corruption and a organized way of dealing with the problem, but try telling her that. She returned hours later and seemed a little fried on drugs. I had remembered that it was her pay day and I asked her about that. "you've gone and bought drugs haven't you" I said telling her there was no point in lying and she nodded indicating that I was right. I straight away asked if she went to Roy Trifford's for it but she said Racheal got it and that she didn't know who from. I was a little suspicious as I had the feeling she was lying. I told her I was going to have a shower and I bolted the door locked before going to the bathroom. I could sense something wasn't right so I turned on the shower but didn't get in. I stayed fully dressed and put my ear to the door and before long I could here her talking. I opened the door slightly and she was on the phone with her back to me. She was saying that I was in the shower now was a perfect time to come. I shut the door and listened and it was only a couple of minutes and I could hear her open the door and start talking to someone. I took 3 deep breaths then opened the door startling Roy Trifford who was all the way in the room with Scotty not far behind. I moved quickly my mission was to get out the door. I somehow managed to get passed Ray and Scotty unchallenged and was about to exit the door when gunny punched me twice in the face. "Is that all you've got" I said as he started to wrestle with me. There was no way I was letting the three of them have me trapped in that room. I wrestled my way out of that room and gunny was trying to lift me over the railing as we were upstairs. Eventually a man and lady in a neighbouring room opened they're door and threatened police. Gunny said "I haven't finish with you cunt" and he ran down the stairs followed by the other two dragging Joanna with them and forcing her into the car. Before long the motel owner Mr Simpson was at my door kicking me out of the motel. I explained that I had just been attacked but he didn't care "I don't need the fucking police here all over my shit "he said. Obviously my stay was not on the books and was cash in hand. I used to stay there regularly and I pleaded that to him but he insisted I had to leave. I couldn't leave Joanna would never know where to find me and Roy Trifford had taken my money and my phone. I decided to just stay and if he wanted me to leave he would have to physically kick me out. I went and had my shower and remembered Joanna rang Racheal's phone from the room phone and I could press last number re-dial. I rang Racheal and told her what had happened. I told her to tell Joanna she was right to còme back "just tell her to trust me I'm not a dog" I said. A few hours past and Joanna returned, Racheal dropped her off. We had sex for the first time and went to sleep. Joanna had robbed a few safes with the career criminal boyfriend Paul and that's what she had been charged for.

CHAPTER 9

Day Tripper

Sydney was blistering cold. It was 3am and the middle of winter when Joanna and myself arrived at Campbelltown train station. We had not planned anything and left Rockhampton in a hurry with little clothing. Rockhampton was still nice and warm as it was in the tropics but in Sydney it was a different story. There was no one organized to pick us up. We had no money, all we could do was try to huddle together to keep warm. We were outside in the wind freezing so I rang John. John and Noel agreed to pick us up but we waited a hour and they didn't come and when I rang back there was no answer. All I could think to do was go to a friend's place Andrew young but it was 25 minutes drive away. I eventually asked a taxi driver how I could get a taxi without money, "was there a way I could pay later" I asked. The taxi driver agreed to allow it if I showed him proper identification. Andrew young and his wife Christine were happy to see us. It was about 4am so they made up a sofa bed for us and we went to bed. The next morning I went to see my accountant to lodge my tax return. Whist I was there I borrowed a few hundred dollars and I rang John and they came and picked us up. After buying amphetamines we headed back to Johns apple orchid out at a town called Oakdale. Later that night John for some reason handed me a large pocket knife and told me to keep it. It was around 2am and john decided to show Joanna up Nattai Lookout.

Nattai lookout overlooked the deepest sunken valley in the southern hemisphere and is 2,522 feet above sea level. I don't know why he wanted to show Joanna as it was dark you couldn't see anything. It was very remote and Joanna became increasingly frightened. She thought I was going to kill her and dump her body. She started saying "please don't hurt me ill do anything" I asked "what are you talking about" and Joanna replied "the knife, I know he gave you the knife to kill me" "don't be silly" I said saying "why would I pay $5000 dollars then kill you" I threw the knife out the window and Joanna eventually settled down but for a while I thought she was going to jump out of the moving car. Next thing I hear John say "look out Noel "while yanking hard left on the steering wheel. In Australia we drive on the left hand side of the road, the middle of the road was to the right. As that happened I felt the car swerve really hard. I looked ahead and saw a car going sideways past us very nearly hitting us head on. I continued to watch the car fish tail side to side out of control eventually hitting a tree. It hit the tree so hard the back wheels came off the ground. Noel jammed on the brakes but because of his brain damage the braking was delayed. When we came to a full stop Joanna was screaming at the top pf her lungs "arrrrrrrh arrrrrrh "John yelled out "go Noel fucking go" Noel jumped on the gas and the car took off. I yelled out "stop "and Noel came to a screeching stop. John yelled "go you fucking idiot". Noel jammed the accelerator to floor driving us back into our seats. I screamed out once more for Noel to stop and he did. John said "what are you going to do man" and I replied "save these peoples lives" "Common Joanna lets go" I said and we jumped out of the car. It was a good few hundred metres back down the road and we ran all the way. We got to the passenger side window and the car was bent like a banana from the impact. The tree was almost in the front cabin of the car. There was a lady with her neck completely slumped forward. her mouth gurgled as she struggled to breath you could tell her neck was broken. John eventually turned up "oh no fuck this "he said "this is bullshit, im getting out of here" and he started to run away. "Call the ambulance John" I yelled "don't you leave these people here to die" but John kept on running then got into the car and drove away. There was a man in the drivers seat of the crashed car. He was starting regain consciousness and he started screaming and shaking the women. Worried about her spinal injury's I tried telling him from the passenger window "common mate don't shake her "I said but he wouldnt stop. I ran around his side of the car and tried to stop him but he just kept screaming and shaking her. Her neck was getting flung all over the place. I grabbed him and ripped him out of the car. "stop it "it told him "settle down" but he kept trying to fight me. I let him go and he immediately raced back to the car and started shaking her again. Worried the cold would slow the ladies heart rate and she would die I quickly took my jumper and shirt off. "Quick put these over the lady "I instructed Joanna. I grabbed hold of the man from behind putting my arms under his arm pits and clenching my fingers together behind his head. I wrapped my legs around his waist and fell back on the ground so he couldn't move. Joanna and I didn't know if ambulances were on the way or not. If no one came soon the lady would die. Joanna monitored her breathing and pulse while I tried to get the man to talk. "oh my god I've killed her "he kept saying" "I tried to ask him "is that your wife" but he kept saying the same thing. Joanna said "she's having trouble breathing". Fearing the lady would die I let the man go. There was no way I could give her CPR in the confined space she was sitting in. Reaching in the drivers side I grabbed hold of her and pulled her out of the car. Once laying flat on the ground her neck wasn't crimped and she seemed to breath better. Joanna was struggling to hold the man back so I instructed her to keep a check on the lady's breathing and pulse while I climbed onto the mans back and tackled him to the ground again. It seemed to take forever but finally we heard sirens coming. "hear that" Joanna said. "everything is going to be fine" I told the man. The ambulances pulled up followed by police. Johns mother turned up in Noels car and she asked me to go switch off the ignition. I was instructed to pull on the steering wheel to lock the steering. It was obvious Johns mother was trying to frame me. After putting the two people in the ambulances police came and recorded my details. John's mother listened very careful to what was said but police said they would take statements at a later stage. The mother then offered Joanna and myself a lift to Johns house. As soon as I got a chance I warned Joanna to be careful. Noel had millions of dollars to lose and it was obvious he ran the people off the road. I was worried the brothers might murder us and say we were driving so Joanna and I left immediately. We walked the 7 kilometres to the next town where I had a cousin called Meghan. Meghan was quite proper and posh and I was a little worried about just turning up there. The sun had came up it must have been 8am and at least the walk had kept us warm which was a relief from the blistering cold. Meghan greeted us at the front door "oh hello Dawrin" she said with a W instead of the R. She was quite nice and I quickly introduced Joanna. "We've been in a car crash" Joanna told her "oh my god come inside you poor things" "Ill make you both a cup of tea "she said as we told her of the accident. She said she thought she heard the sirens go past early hours of the morning. When we were finished chatting Meghan suggested we should stay down Wollongong with my aunty Yvonne. "She will enjoy the company now that George has died."Meghan pointed out that she was alone and had been for quite some time. I took my Aunty Yvonne's number and gave her a call. She said she'd be glad to have us so we headed straight to the train station. Campbelltown to Wollongong by train was quite a journey. We had to travel all the way to Sydney then it was about 2 hours from Sydney to Wollongong. Aunty Yvonne lived in the best housing commission spot I had ever seen. She had un obstructed beach front views out her lounge room window. She lived on Bellambi beach which is now a Japanese golf course from what im told. My memory of aunty Yvonne and uncle George were quite different as they were the laid back weed smoking hippy type. Uncle George was in rock bands and died of natural causes at 49 worn out from drug's and alcohol abuse but he was happy about it. Yvonne hadn't change and she welcomed us with open arms. "Oh Darren" "its so good to see you" she said with her well read English accent "do come in" she said. "who's this" she asked and I introduced Joanna. Like with Meghan we chatted over cups of tea and I asked again if it was ok if we stayed. "the two of you can stay as long as you like "she said which made me feel relieved. I could recover from the traumas and head back to work I thought. I put Joanna on the train about a week later. She had to go meet her ex boyfriend who was being released from deer park prison.

Joanna sang all the way to the train station so I knew she wouldnt be coming back. She used to say I read into everything looking for some sort of sign and I guess she knew I would get the message. She rang wanting a motel room when she got to deer park and I told her to go find one that she wanted and ring me back with the motel phone number. Once Joanna rang with the number I put on my business class voice and rang up. "yes its Darren Russell calling from Sydney im wanting to book a room for a Ms Joanna Martini" I said "sorry the rooms are all booked out" The man said. He told me the entire motel was full off police in town for something suspicious. I asked for the phone number to another motel one that was relatively close and I warned Joanna of the police presence in town. Knowing Joanna and her boyfriend police probably didn't recover the money from the last heist. Intel from the prison would have overheard the phone calls. Calls about how they would meet the day he was being released. I told Joanna that she need to lie low in the motel for a few days. If police were trying to follow them to the money she had to wear them down "What do I do" she asked and I told her that police wouldnt be able to stay in the motels for too long. There budget wouldn't allow it and they would eventually leave thinking there was no money to go to. Police were probably already watching Joanna. I rang the motel up the road and used the same business class voice. It worked they booked a room for Ms Joanna Martini in town for business for a few days. He booked it under my name and took my details. I never heard from Joanna about what had happened but the motel owner rang chasing the money for the motel as Her and the ex boyfriend stayed 4 nights eating lobster and charging it to the room. I quickly pointed out that I only booked the room and that I never said I was paying. Police rang me and I was right John and Noel were trying to make out I was driving the car. I called Charmaine from Mastermyne to see about a job. I started chatting her up all over again. Sheridan had fried my brain so much I couldn't remember meeting her in the motel in Mackay. Now she had a number to contact me she started ringing every couple of days "Does it look like a job for superman" I would always say when I realized it was her. She said on this occassion "no Darren im ringing for a chat "she asked where I was and if I could paint her a picture so I told her I was in a house overlooking the beach. I told her there was about 6 guys on surfboards surfing just outside the front window and that I was playing guitar with my Aunt. I asked if she would like to hear a song and I played a song from skid row. A few days later a company called Ground Consolidation had given me a job at Tahmoor colliery. They came and interviewed me at home after seeing my resume. They had to do a lot of explosive work and didn't have many people with explosives experience apply. Explosives in underground coal mines are rarely used and its a specialized field. Ground Consolidation didn't tell me that I was the boss. The only indication was I was given a different hard hat to everyone else. My hard hat said elite on it and it had a No1 sticker on the back. They had employed a few old deputy's that hadn't worked underground for 10 and 15 years. Deputy's are mining bosses like a shift boss in charge of the men and everyone including me assumed they would be the bosses. We didn't realize that they weren't appointed as deputy's by the manager for that job. We all went underground to start our first shift. No one really knew what we were to be doing as we were given very rough instructions. We were told a section of conveyor belt structure around the underground storage bin was to be removed and that we were to shoot the roof out with explosives to make room for a much bigger storage bin. The size of the longwall machine had increased the output of coal and they now needed a much larger storage bin. The storage bin wasn't going to be rounder it was to be twice as tall so the roof needed blasting so it would fit. Colin Medley was the deputy that hadn't worked underground for 15 years. Being a deputy we thought he was our leader so we all followed him for instructions. Cole Medley had the men start unbolting the conveyor belt structure and pull it to pieces. When they asked where to put the pieces he had them carrying it around the corner and stacking it in our way. Other men he told to start unbolting all the metal roof supports that held the roof up. Pretty soon we had all these men walking around under un supported roof. Roof that is old and un supported is dangerous and It becomes what they call drummy. Drummy roof means air or water or both has separated the layers of rock. You hit the roof with a hammer or drill steel if it sounds solid it goes doonk doonk a solid deep or high penetrating sound. if its drummy it goes thump thump a much blunter sounding hollow noise and you can tell it's only penetrated the thin layers. Drummy roof will break off in slabs and a 2 feet thick layer is enough to break your neck. I hit the roof with a drill steal it was drummy. Cole Medley was undoing a nut of a roof bolt and as he was undoing it I could see the roof creeping down. I yelled "get out of the way "and pulled him back into supported roof. A big chunk fell out and crashed to the floor right where he was standing. He went to scold me for man handling him but I fought back angrily and man handled him some more. I told him just how big a mistake he was making and it must have been crushing for him as it was in front of a dozen men. Medley was known as a tough guy in his day but his day had long gone. Rumour was he killed a bloke underground after they were revealed for fucking each others wives. Apparently he snuck up behind the guy and smashed his head in with a steal bar. They found the guy dead from head injury's but they could never prove it. I pointed out 1. all the belt structure needs to go somewhere most likely it needs to go out of the mine and not be stacked in our roadways blocking the machinery getting to us. The structure needs to go on a trailer so it can be removed by machines as we were installing a different size structure. Number 2. taking out all roof supports means we will not be able to drill the blast holes as we cant work under un supported roof. We will put back all roof support then drill the blast holes I told everyone. I then made a example of all the roof bolters and hoses laying near the work area and I pointed out what they were there for. Roof bolters are drills on a air leg (air hydraulic ram) I told the men to split into 2 groups 1 group run the air and water hoses for the bolters and start drilling the blast holes. The other half were told to bolt the roof supports back up. One Idiot said "then what do we do "To which I replied "ill tell you tomorrow" and laughed "that will be enough for one shift" I told him. After that shift I went and saw the mine manager. I explained that no one had given us real instructions. I told him what I had done and asked what needed to be done there advising him that at the rate we were moving it would take a day or two. "a day or two for what "he asked "for the roof cavity to be blasted out." And I told him that job was almost done.

The manager was impressed but said they had more work to do which was the ground consolidation of the roof to support the longwall relocation he told me. Ground Consolidation meant pumping a glue into the broken drummy roof to glue the layers and broken bits back together. "Can I have a look and set up to do that job as well "I asked asking if it was ok to work overtime that day. He pointed out they were going to be hiring men to work there permanent but I told him I was happy contracting. I went and found all the equipment needed to glue the roof and I had it transported to the work area. It was going to be a huge job as the roof was badly broken. Tahmoor was notorious for burying its long wall machine. Its worth more then 20 million dollars maybe 50 million may be closer. If it gets buried again the mine would close. I continued to work overtime and a double shift every day. Trouble was I didn't realize no one was booking it in on time sheets. When it came to the first payday which was a full eleven days from when we started. I should have received around $1800 but I received the same as everyone else. $1000 that was what they paid me for seven 12 hour shifts. The other men only did five 8 hour days with no overtime. I rang the director furious and then they made it worse by asking me how many hours did I work Monday Tuesday Wednesday Thursday to Sunday. After all that he then said "here ill forward you to a pay clerk". The pay clerk did the same thing and asked for every single day and the hours I worked and then forwarded me to someone else. 20 minutes of this and I was blowing my top and about to explode. They passed me on one more time and I just hollered "put the director back on the line". I told him that I would not go back to work until they fixed my pay. "Please don't do that" "we want to fix it" he said. Before asking "how many hours on Monday all over again. I just said "I've already told you and 3 other people you ring when its fixed and ill go back to work. I went immediately and rang Charmaine "got a job for superman "I said like I always did and I rang Brett Gorome from ready workforce as well. I didn't want to put all my eggs in one basket as I was thinking it was all a deliberate setup. Maybe I had done too much work. Maybe that was it. Maybe I had shortened the life of there contract by getting the job done fast I was thinking. If that was the case it would be easy to believe that it was deliberate as I was basically putting them out of work. They were laughing at me at first so I rang the CFMEU Mining Union and spoke to Spotty White. Spotty assured me not to worry and that he would get it all sorted out. He wanted to meet me at 3pm so I found out where the union office was and went there. Un be known to me Spotty white meant meet at the mine site. The mine site was 50 minutes drive away from Wollongong and I had no idea. All he said was meet with him at 3pm. I had no car I hitchhiked to work and got lifts. Transport was what I needed the whole pay for. When I found out Spotty white went to the mine but didn't sort it out because I wasn't there it sent me whacko. I went off my nut "what the fuck do you need me for" I told him "you had all the details, you wrote them down." "you fucking useless cunt "I called him. The boss of ground consolidation wasn't at the mine. He was in Newcastle 3 hours away. I gave them heaps of abuse over the phones as I couldn't help it. All the dumb shit I had put up with lately was sending me nuts and I taken enough crap to do me a life time. When I watched TV I got into the boxing and used to watch a lot of it. Shannon Taylor the Bulli blaster had just lost his world title bout against Oscar Delahoya. I went to school with Shannon Taylor and his sister and I watched all his fights. After recognizing him as soon as he walked into Bellambi hotel I had to say g'day. It was a Saturday Late August 2002 horse race day and I was having a few bets. It was in the paper that he lost his fight because he was on cocaine. He kept looking and nodding at me and I nodded back. I had 4 big chunky gold rings and a wicked Nike reversible jacket and Nike herachis. I guess I must have looked like a drug dealer. He kept pumping money into the pokie machines Hundreds after hundreds of dollars until he had none left. He had to come my way to go to the ATM bank. Straight away I said "are you Shannon Taylor" "yeah bud" he replied. I went to shake his hand but it almost seemed like he didn't want to shake it. "Gentle" he said "your not going to hurt me are ya "he said as he gave me a really timid handshake. I thought the guy was crazy being scared of me and knew he must of been joking. He didn't appear like the staunch competitor he was in the ring. I felt like I could take him on but in reality he could punch me to death easily. I would later realize why he was so frightened to shake hands. Your hands are always sore as the best punching bags are hard like a tree trunk from the packed down saw dust. The hard punching bag snaps your hands back after contact and is more like hitting real bone. Because you are punching all the time you can punch harder then most and your fingers are hair lined fractured all the time and very sore. Big calices end up on the outside of your knuckles and Being a boxer people are always poking punches at you. Some people just think "hey I can take him" and start swinging on you. I told Shannon I was a big fan pointing out I went to Bulli primary school. "you were a year younger and your sister a year older "I said. I used to go roller skating with them on weekends. He was a nice well mannered sort of bloke. That was a life changing moment for me and I started training immediately. Just shadow boxing and getting used to poking the punches out. Moving like a boxer up and down and in and out was obviously important so I practiced it. It wasn't long before I started bouncing 2 tennis balls off the wall simultaneously. Most wouldnt believe me but Id catch both balls at the same time. I did that to build up both my peripheral vision and hand eye co-ordination. We did lots of martial arts when I was 16 and 17 but boxing would prove to be way better. No more taking shit for me my mind was made up the next time someone pissed me off I was coming out fighting and all I had to do was practise. If you do anything often enough you'll get good at it. Believe it or not I had rang my mother and father. Both Charmaine and Brett Gorome had work back in Queensland for me and I needed a lift or someone to put me on the plane or bus. It was 2000 perhaps 3000 kilometres back to work and I had no idea they had been asking my Aunty Yvonne about me. My aunty Yvonne had kept saying to me that I needed to go on a government pension. She kept trying to get me to see a doctor and I guess she was lonely and wanted me to stay there with her for good. I fed her and kept her safe at night but trying to make out I was head case just wasn't on as I was highly skilled. I worked all over the country and was in the prime of my life. There was no way I was going on a pension. She had been secretly plotting with my parents and tricking them and Aunty Yvonne had them thinking I had mental problems. She had done this knowing how my mum would react as my parents would likely put me in a nut house. They came to pick me up but kept carrying on about seeing a doctor. They carried on so much I told them to fuck off. "Darren please see a doctor Son "my mum kept saying "what for is he gonna give me my pay "I said "how the fuck is he going to get me to Queensland "I argued before telling them to fuck off and leaving on foot. Up the road was a guy I had bought some speed off, Sambo they called him. After telling him about what had just happened he asked where it was my parents lived. I told him forster up the coast. It just happened that he bought his drugs from up past Newcastle which was half way. "I have to drive up that way tomorrow "he said. He told me if my parents had gone home I could drive with him. When I went back to aunty Yvonne's they had left and gone home so the next morning I left with Sambo. I had rang the parents the night before and got them to meet me a hour and half south of there place so I had a 2 and half hour trip north with the Bellambi drug dealer. We had stacks in common he was about 15 or 20 years older. He would have been around 50 but he was pretty cool. He had a young daughter that still lived with him and she had a little girl. That and serving drugs to young people and people from all walks of life had kept him in touch with things to do with everything. It seemed to have kept him young. He wore nice sporting clothes and I felt really comfortable with him. He let me in on a few secrets. One that he scored his drugs from 3 ex police officers. He confided that he was actually frightened of them. They always made him stay overnight and would scare the hell out of him. We agreed corrupt coppers are very Dangerous and we had both watched blue murder. Blue murder was a real life movie about Australian police officers that were selling drugs and murdering people. It just so happened that they might have been involved and the same police officers. Sambo was pleading with me to ring my parents and tell them I was staying in Newcastle over night. "ill drive you up tomorrow "he offered. I felt for him and thought about it. I just didn't need to get murdered so I told him no. He started begging "please im scared man "I think there gonna kill me bro "he said. I rang my parents phone but they had already left. I felt bad. If I stayed with him it may save his life and we could make out my parents wanted to know where I was staying. That would keep us safe I guessed as the cops would know someone would notice us missing. "Just tell them you have to pick me up in the morning" "bluff them" I said telling him to ring me off they're phone as re assurance. "Actually ring me "I told him but he never rang. I never heard from him again. At the parents house I kept phoning both Ground Consolidation and the union. I would leave abusive messages on the answering machine while my father drove me nuts. He kept getting me to repeat what had happened. "what did they do" he would ask several times a day While Mum kept saying "you need to see a doctor son" "I want him to see a doctor Mick" she would say to my father. Mick is what she called him although his named is Mark. Drinking seemed to numb it all and it made me very happy. I shadow boxed in the window as I could see my reflection. The phone rang, it was Joanna "boy am I glad to hear your voice" she said. Lane from Vaccro had passed on my parents number. Vaccro was a young re offenders outreach program as Joanna was in custody and she said she was hanging for a cigarette. I told her I was headed back to work in Queensland. "wanna come" I asked. She wanted me to get her out but I just didn't have the connections. After a while the phone cut out so I kept drinking my vodka and lemonade. A few minutes went past and the phone rang. "hay baby girl" I said before saying what I wanted to do to her. To my surprise It wasn't her. "I beg your pardon" the girl said. "who is this" I asked. It was Charmaine so I played along with her. "yeah I know im only joking" I told her trying to make out I knew it was her. I asked if she was married and she said "no" "your not the bosses daughter are you" I joked. We had another great conversation but again I thought the call was work related as I was a little slow when it came to girls. When a girl comes onto me I don't realize until I think it over later. I had 2 jobs to go to one was to drive the shearer at Kenmare mine and the other started 10 days before that with Mastermyne. My parents harassed me every day to see a doctor and I was angry about not receiving my pay from ground consolidation. After 5 days at my parents place it was time to leave. I had seen doctors for them but there is little the doctors can do. My parents were driving me all the way to Queensland to a town called Oaky creek. I didn't want to go with my parents but they insisted.

CHAPTER 10

The Royal Run Around

My father always took the back way when he travelled. We were headed towards Queensland, the obvious way to drive would be up the coast. Instead he always travelled inland meaning you have less services available. My mother kept saying "lay down son you need the rest" So I would lay down. Then my father would ask again "what happened with Ground Consolidation "it was driving me crazy. Eventually I exploded making them stop the car. I got out to have a well earned cigarette but they drove off before I could grab my lighter. "Go mick "I heard mum scream as my father jumped on the accelerator and went. I never saw them again for about 4 hours after a Police car came and picked me up. They had driven over 120 kilometres to a town called Warialda. In Warialda they went to police and as a result police came to get me. I wasn't in trouble police came as where they left me was very remote and Police were concerned as I was left there without any food and water. They were also worried I might hitchhike as there was a fork in the road. They assumed I wouldnt know which way to go or which way I would be taken if there was foul play. When the police re united me with my parents my parents wouldnt allow me to get in the car. Frustrated I threw my lighter at the ground so hard it exploded with a bang! My mother then turned to police saying "aren't you going to stop him" but I had done nothing wrong so police said "he hasn't done anything". My Father handed me $200 and said I couldn't get in the car. I think the money was so I could make my own way as they put my bags out on the ground. I was truly annoyed and overturned a couple of huge concrete pots. The pots were so big it took 3 counsel workers to turn them upright. Police charged me for wilful damage as I smashed the handsets on two telephone boxes as well. That's when I realized I must have a decent punch. I was holding the plastic handset and punching the wall and both handsets broke in half and police eventually escorted me out of town. They drove me to the city limits from where I hitchhiked to a town called Inverell. I started drinking with the $200 my father had given me. I was hyperactive and really fit from riding mountain bikes and boxing. I had been riding in Wollongong with a cycling group called party pigs and they would ride around 180 kilometres on a Sunday afternoon before drinking at North Wollongong hotel. Full of pent up rage it was a recipe for disaster and It wasn't long before I was in a fight. Some fool had jammed all the pool balls we were playing with down the holes in the table. "you took my turn "he said as he grabbed all the balls and quickly sunk them in the pockets. I was quick as lighting "crack crack" with the blunt end of my pool cue punching it into his face. If you swing it like a bat it only has the weight of pool cue in it but If you jab it out longways you can get your body weight behind it and deliver a much harder blow. I hit him a couple more times before the publican grabbed him and threw him out. My father had paid by credit card for a room for me so You could say I was a guest. But in all honesty I think he grabbed him rather then try to grab hold of me. The next morning my parents turned up to pick me up it was September 11 911 and aeroplanes had just flown through the buildings in America. "I said there was going to be a war" I told my father "what war "my father said. Once again all they cared about was getting me to see a doctor. What was important was getting me to work like they promised. When I grabbed my bags and went to get in the car they said "not until you see a doctor". I agreed I would see a doctor but asked if I could have a cigarette first. "Not until you see a doctor" they said. I was furious but had to keep my cool one outburst and they would call police again. "take me to one "I asked but they didn't know where one was. Starving hungry and hanging for a cigarette I told them the hospital would be a likely place. We drove to the hospital but when the nurse asked what was wrong I told her the truth. I told her about work ripping me off in my pay and that that was making me angry. That along with my parents continual harassment about seeing a doctor and making me repeat myself. The nurse said they couldn't schedule me to see a doctor for those reasons as they is no way to treat me. I wasn't injured so they told me to go away. Not good enough for my parents they insisted they weren't moving until I saw a doctor. There was nothing I could do and I screamed with frustration. All I wanted to do was have something to eat and a cigarette. My parents took off to the police station and police arrested me. They held me for hours and gave me the usual drill and I knew the police weren't going to let me go until I calmed down. The sergeant eventually handed me my bags saying "its in the bag son" "what's in the bag" I asked but he simply said again "its in the bag" and told me to go. When I got outside there was no car or parents waiting for me. It took me quite a while before I realized I had to look in my bag. I was angry again as I was still waiting for something to eat and a cigarette. Dad had left a envelope with another $200 in my bag. I went and got a feed and cigarettes and a taxi to the next town Glen Innes as there were no buses or trains out of Inverell. I was marooned so a taxi was my only option. When I got to Glen Innes I had just enough money left to buy a bus ticket to Brisbane. Brisbane was 500 kilometres away and the only place that had a transport route to where I was going as there was still 1000 kilometres I had to travel after that. It was about 1 pm September 11 2002 and the bus I was to catch wasn't until 4:30am the next morning. I was going to have to go without food and drink for over 21 hours as I had no money until I got to Brisbane. With the change I had left I rang my fathers message bank as his phone was switched off. My parents had never left me stranded in my life so I left messages saying where I was. I honestly thought they would come and get me as I told them I had no food. My father called police and told them I needed medical attention. He told them this because the police said that unless I was breaking the law or in need of medical treatment they couldn't do anything. He told them I was suicidal and had a knife. Police drew there guns at me when they approached and they then interrogated me making me explain my every move. I had to explain the whole saga which took about 40 minutes. The reminder of it all made me very angry but I had to stay as calm as possible or I was in serious trouble. There was a giant prison in Glen Innes I could see it in the distance and it scared the hell out me as I was getting really tired. My bags were heavy and I had walked up into town about 1 kilometre to try and organize money from Centrelink. At Centrelink no one would help me. There was no crisis type of payment that I knew of or they could give me. I terminated my payments from that day saying I was starting work the following day. Terminating my Centrelink allowance meant they had to pay me what was owing and I would receive money in 2 working days. The only trouble was I had no ATM cards to withdraw it as I had new ones on order. The police came and harassed me again 2 more times as my father managed to get the same crew to come twice. Then when the shift changed and new police came on duty he tricked them into doing the same thing. I couldn't sleep. I tried but couldn't settle and I chain smoked my cigarettes and was now without. I've never been so angry in my life. When the bus came I couldn't get on it. If I left my parents wouldnt know where I was and would worry. I really thought they would come so I made a decision to stay meaning I now had to go without food and drink for 2 days. When I arrived at Glen Innes I managed to speak to Charmaine from Mastermyne. I told her I was having trouble with my parents and I should of taken her offer for help as the following day I was starving. I walked back into town and found a homeless shelter for woman that was ran by Nuns and after telling them my story they invited me in for a meal. They explained that a lot of the woman were victims of violence and scared of men so I was on my best behaviour. The next morning at 4:30am another bus to Brisbane came. I showed the driver the ticket from the day before and said I missed the bus. He let me get on and 6 hours later I was in Brisbane. I had to walk a long way to a commonwealth bank and my bags were weighing me down. They weren't bags that were meant for carrying long distance. Eventually I had enough money to catch a plane so I got a taxi cab to Brisbane airport. It felt so good to get out of the heat and in the airport air-conditioning. The airport was packed. Because of the 911 tragedy in America and planes weren't moving anywhere. I couldn't carry the bags any further so I left them laying beside the Telstra payphones. Hanging for a cigarette and a drink I raced upstairs to where the shops were and I grabbed 2 cans of VB beer and change for the smoke machine. By the time I had got back outside to where you could smoke one beer was gone. I walked out the automatic doors and there was a picket line of demonstrators on my right hand side. To my left side was news and TV cameras and some reporters. "hey what's going on" I asked one of the union blokes. "Ansett Airline has collapsed and all the workers cant get any money" the bloke said. Seeing me standing out front of the demonstrators must have made it look as if I was the leader. Before I knew it there was a TV camera and microphone in my face. The reporter spoke into the microphone briefly outlining the situation. He then asked what I had to say about the dilemma and put the microphone in front of my mouth. I had a beer in one hand and a smoke in the other "the worker's cant get any money to feed there families or pay the mortgage and bills "I said. I then went on to say "the government should step in like when Oakdale Colliery went bust and assist the workers with immediate Centrelink payments. Oakdale Colliery was a Coal Mine who's owners gambled the men's wages on the stock market and lost causing them to go into bankruptcy. The government closed a entire branch of Centrelink and re opened for the workers only. When I finished my cigarette and walked away a guy in a suit followed me. He stopped me and asked me who I was. He then asked what I was doing now "looking for a payphone as I need to call my dad" I told him. He handed me his phone "here use mine "he said. I asked him if he was sure and he told me it was Rupert Murdoch's phone as Rupert owned the news. I rang dad and told him I was calling from Rupert Murdoch's phone. He thought I was delusional especially after saying I was on the news. "Can you buy me a airfare to Rockhampton" I asked him but he told me he was coming to pick me up "go find a motel near the Airport then ring me" he said. All around the airport is industrial areas, offices and workshops. Today they have airport hotels but 20 years ago I don't think there was. I went to get my bags and the bomb squad had petitioned them off. "everybody back" "back please sir "the soldier said to me. "what's going on with my bags "I asked as another soldier who was scanning them with some sort of explosives and ammunitions detector. "Are they your bags sir "he asked before commanding me to a pat down. He frisked searched me up against the wall then asked me abruptly what the bags were doing there. I told him to look around "there are bags everywhere" I said. "Its a airport man there's hundreds of bags" I told him. He was just picking on my bag because it was a camouflaged army bag. I got my bags and grabbed another taxi. Another $40 wasted but I arrived at the Hamilton Hotel Motel. I bought 2 vodkas and lemonade and $10 change to ring my father. My father asked so many questions that it used up my money and the payphone started beeping indicating it was low and required more "gets some change and ring back son ring back "my parents said so I did. They did this over and over tricking me into thinking they were coming. They just wanted to know the address and to bankrupt me so I couldn't move. Realizing this I rang work to let them know I was in Brisbane. I wanted to Ask Charmaine could she organize a plane ticket for me but Marie another secretary answered. Marie said that Charmaine wasn't there she was getting a tooth pulled. I remember her saying she had a sore tooth when she rang my parents house. Being a gentlemen I offered to pay to have it removed as she couldn't afford it. "ask Lee to pay and take it from my wages" "it has to come out" I said. "Why do you want to speak to Charmaine so bad Darren" Marie teased. The other girls must have known about us as Marie kept on teasing me. I was tired and said "she was the only one that would understand". I had already told her about the trouble I was having with my parents and I couldn't go through having to explain it again. Marie told me my job was gone and that I had been replaced as my parents had rang and said I was in Hospital. I had a nervous breakdown she said. Embarrassed I pleaded with her but it was too late the job was gone. I told Marie about the other job I had with ready workforce and she advised me that that was gone as well. Mastermyne had rang Brett Gorome thinking they were doing me favour. They advised him that I was in hospital and I was quickly replaced. As I stumbled away from the phone two police officers stopped me. They searched me and my bags and interrogated me and the two officers made me tell them the whole story. Keeping a person awake for long periods and asking them questions is a form of torture. I had had enough and I decided to give up fighting. I went into the motel and told the owner my story. He agreed to ring my parents to tell them that I wanted to go to hospital. I had no money left and was starving and very tired. My parents wouldnt help me get to the hospital I was dumb founded. It was 40 kilometres to the hospital I couldn't walk there on foot. Eventually my parents agreed to get me a room but just the room no food. While I was sleeping police burst into the room after reports that I was suicidal and had a rope and a knife. The interrogation was starting to send me crazy. having to relive everything that made me angry cant of been good. After the police went the owner cooked me some sausages and boiled vegetables. I ate as much as I could but it wasn't very good. He paid a taxi to drive me to the hospital the following morning where hospital staff had also received calls from my parents. Everything they were told was a lie. I felt better after sleeping and I explained the whole sorry story thinking it would be the last time. To my surprise they didn't want to admit me. "your just a little tired and need a good feed "the nurse said. She rang my father to tell him the news and he exploded. She told him to stop having me harassed by police and that it was putting me in danger and he hung up the phone. As I was walking away she called me back. She was worried that if she let me go I would be in danger from my father. The nurse asked me would I like to stay and I agreed. She told me it would have to be in the mental health section because it had facility's better suited. I would have my own room and access to the gym and unlike the other patients I could come and go as I pleased. "we'll run some tests and prove your not crazy" she told me so I settled in.

CHAPTER 11

3 Of A Kind

Whilst in hospital I trained morning and night. Mostly punching in time with hip hop beats. Staying with the beat helped maintain stamina and I would punch the whole hour. During the Day I drank with strippers. I danced on stage and took my clothes off. I took them off to Black Sabbath a couple of times but I don't have the credentials to be a stripper, It was my birthday. The girls had given me a show as they new my birthday was coming up but they hardly performed during the day as there was no one there except me, me and the occasional perv. Weekends may have been a little different but during the week I had the girls to myself. I got down and dirty by day and back to hospital for dinner at night. The other patients thought it was magic. They would trip out over me leaving every day. They thought I escaped daily as they were locked in and couldn't leave. They heard voices and talked to walls and all were scared of the infra red and the planes flying through the buildings had really set the other patients off as a lot of them blamed the Americans for the voices they were hearing. They thought Americans had technology to listen to and control there thoughts. Don't get me wrong im not a critic I made really good friends in there. They thought I was special as I explained things differently. I boxed and drank with strippers as well but was in a mental facility. They thought it was cool and it kind of was. Bob was on lithium and hated it. It controlled his muscles and on occasions they went like jelly and he had no control. He would not be able to control when he cried and sometimes when he went to the toilet. It didn't make sense as without lithium he seemed normal. He used to talk about EMP electro magnetic pulse guns. The EMP were weapons of mass destruction Bob would say and tell me all about them and in theory it worked. It fired a lightening bolt or bullets made from electricity. It also had a switch and you clicked it to make it fire big long electric bolts or sparks. The idea was that it would fuck the computers and burn out wiring and shit like that and I guess that made the doctors scared. Its not safe to be intelligent unless you have a certificate. Being intelligent around people certified to be will get you in trouble. I was at a party with a chick from home and away one time, I cant remember the name as she was only on there a couple of months. I sat and talked with her and her brick laying boyfriend. Everyone else that was there was a Uni student and they encouraged everyone to boycott vegemite. They wanted it boycotted as craft owned vegemite and it was owned by Americans. I think it was to do with American mining company's or something like that. My cousins boyfriend was a devoted greeny. He was speaking about the boycott "everyone gather round" he said. He started waffling on about coal mining. He was saying the remaining coal could only last 40 to 50 years he said it would be all gone and totally used up. That would mean we had to stop mining coal now. I pointed out there were dozens of coal seams we could mine that were at all different depths under the ground. Some only 3 ft thick and others 30 or 40 metres high to the roof. I explained that some was not quite ready. I also explained some was a little old with not enough gas and oil content. We only mine 1 coal seam usually when we mine in Australia. There's only one other that I've mined and it was very volcanic. He got very angry and started telling me all about his education but I pointed no amount of certificates would make him right. Hospital eventually discharged me about one week later. My father had said after I had gone to hospital I could go back to work but there was no work for me. He wouldnt give me any money for a train ticket to Rockhampton either. Eventually I got money from Centrelink but I had to stay at bobs a couple of days. Once in Rockhampton I secured a job with Central Highlands Mining but I fought with the boss and kicked his hard hat around. The boss guy was a bludger and into industrial sabotage. The mine had got us to dig up some water mains on the surface and after locating where the pipes were leaking we started digging them up with a backhoe. I was carefully trying to guide his bucket on the digger so he wouldnt damage any pipes but it was no use. We were only supposed to be there 3 days as that's all the work there was. Smashing the water pipes in more places then one would secure us more work so that's what he did. I couldn't believe my eyes. Was this for real I was thinking. He got the backhoe and just dug into the standpipe that had several pipelines branching off it. "Wooooo you fucking idiot" I screamed out but it didn't matter to him. He actually shook the bucket side to side breaking half the pipes that were coming out of the stand pipe. This caused everything to need replacing. We would have to dig the whole thing up and replace it all and that would take a weeks maybe a month who knows for sure. Fighting at work was instant dismissal but I didn't hesitate. I ripped him out of the cab and threw him around a bit before walking off. That was it for working for Central highlands. On the way past the offices I ran into Lee Beckart from Mastermyne. "What ya doing Demo" he asked so I told him about the fight. "why don't you come and work for me" he said. He told me to take two days off and get as drunk as I wanted to so I did. I started drinking first thing in the morning drinking VB beer and vodka and lemonade. I would drink two schooners of beer then two vodka then two beers and it was around 2pm and the bar phone rang. It was Charmaine asking for me and she said I had to have a coal board medical. She said I had to have it at 3pm in a town called middle mount. Middle mount was approximately one hour drive and didn't have a car. "You don't have a car" Charmaine said sounding as if she was concerned I couldn't make it. "you just leave it up to superman" "ill fly there" I joked. I turned to these guys I didn't know and offered them a bottle of scotch and a carton of beer for a lift and luckily they agreed. When we got back I was standing at the bar and three guys approached me "have you signed the visitors book "one asked. "what visitors book" I replied. They asked me again and I said "do you work here" but they replied no. They kept asking so then I questioned if it was a joke or had I worked with them before. Again no was they're reply. Eventually I started getting angry. I told them if they didn't go away or if they asked me one more time about the visitors book I would bash them. They laughed and asked me again "have you signed the visitors book". I already had the smallest one picked out. After quickly drinking down the last of my vodka I turned and grabbed the smallest by the shoulders. Two head-butts and he fell straight to the floor. As I went to hit the next guy I was hit by the third really hard smashing my cheek bone. Now laying flat on my back I didn't have time to cover up. Before I knew it there were two heads leaning over with there arms back to punch me. As they lent down I unloaded 4 punches from off the floor and they both fell to the ground. Quickly jumping to my feet I sat one of them up against the bar and drilled his head with at least 9 punches. There was now one of the other guys getting to his feet so I started smashing his head with a pool ball. My nose was broken as one managed to land a punch whilst I was on the floor. My eyes started swelling and before long I was unable to see. I got one of the spectators to walk me home which was luckily just at the back of the club. It turned out the manager had set me up as I had punched him several times the night before. The juke box had ripped me off $5 and when I complained the manager was very disrespectful saying "fuck off dickhead". He was a real big guy called bully so I offered him outside and gave him a hiding. The morning after fighting the 3 blokes I was a mess. I was covered in blood. The food mess was full of men when I went in. Straight away I was looking for guys from the fight but they weren't there. The kitchen manager came to speak to me saying the same three guys had roughed him up and damaged his pushbike. He congratulated me and told me from then on I was first. "what do you mean" I asked. He told me in the future all the men could stay locked outside until I had first pick of all the food. There was 250 men in that camp. I had 4 fights in 6 weeks with a total of seven men. I went from being a wimp to the top of the food chain.

CHAPTER 12

Root 666

I won the fight but I turned up for work with 2 black eyes, a broken nose, a smashed cheekbone and 2 broken fingers. "No way Demo "Lee Beckhart said as he spotted me walking into the meeting. "You cant work like that Demo". The rule was you couldn't work underground with stitches so I told him "that's why I didn't get my face stitched up". There was a big gash under my right eye that was still bleeding. Lee Insisted I couldn't work like that but the mining officials disagreed. They knew if I didn't work Mastermyne would sack me so they allowed me to work. They did this on the condition I stopped working if I got any headaches as my eyes were badly haemorrhaged. I drove a front end loader underground a Eimco 130 they call them. They're basically a diesel powered low front end loader except you sit on the side of the machine instead of in the middle. Because I was underground and in a confined space the diesel fumes were stinging my eyes and after 5 or 6 hours of this I was actually crying. A bloke called Pughy offered to swap jobs so I could be in a well ventilated area so I worked on the longwall take off building roof supports. I worked the full 13 hours and did that every day for 6 days. Lee eventually told me to take a day off then work another 6. We had finished the Longwall relocation ahead of schedule and that meant a bonus of $3000 each. Everyone except me got paid the bonus. On the last day Lee Beckart told me to take a particular machine underground and move a heap of cable reels. The machine was broken but because I didn't find the damaged component in my inspections I was blamed. Im not a diesil fitter trained in finding damages like that but he was right. I could have checked if the reeler was working before I went underground. Personally I think I was set up but that cant be proven. I was now also out of a job again but so were a heap of others. While having beers up the pub prior to starting the contract with Mastermyne I got into a conversation with a SBD mining services boss. They needed to employ a heap of men but the camp where we all slept was full and they couldn't get rooms for them. No rooms meant they couldn't put anyone on or if they did they would have to house them a hour and a half away in Middlemount. I obtained a list of men that had also lost there jobs and took it to SBD Mining services. I told them we had rooms already in our names and had just been made redundant. SBD employed the lot of us. I was so happy as SBD mining services had a 2 year contract there at Oaky Creek and that meant as long as I behaved I would be in work for the next two years. They even gave me a car to drive so I immediately hung up my punching bag and settled in. Once working with SBD it wasn't hard for me to move up through the ranks as the manpower they were using was mostly younger blokes that didn't have the experience I had. I had done things in my supply driving to speed up everything we were doing. I told the men to never drive around with a empty loader. I towed a trailer with supplies into the mine and every time I came out my bucket was full of rock or anything that had to go to the surface. I made sure everyone did the same and it helped speed things up. As a result SBD promoted me to shift boss but it was short lived. Whilst at the previous job the men I was working with had been told I had just had a nervous breakdown. They were also told I had diabetes or things to that effect and rumours had started to spread. My father then interfered. My mother was obsessed with me taking epilepsy medication and she would make my father ring up my employers to see if I was taking the tablets. I didn't ever have epilepsy as the doctors could never ever find the unique brain wave to diagnose me with the condition. The doctors had merely said to my parents that they think I had had a epileptic style convulsion and if they continued I would be brain damaged. Before I knew bosses had me in the office wanting to know what medication I was on. I explained that I wasn't on any medication but my father had told them I would denie it. The SBD bosses believed my father and they stopped me from operating all machinery which rendered me useless. It was frustrating as I had to watch all these in experienced people operate the machines knowing I could do a better job. It also bothered me because every time I would even try to get on a machine someone would stop me and say "no you don't Demo "and I guess I didn't like people telling me what to do. I got doctors to examine me and write to the bosses explaining that I wasn't on any medication but it didn't work. Angry I flogged that punching day and night. I would hit it for at least a hour in the morning waking everyone up like a alarm clock. There was 250 men at that camp. Of a night time I would hit it for hours drinking vodka cruisers while I did it. It wasn't long before I was in another fight. Blokes would see me hitting the bag and think that I think im tough and they would wait until they see me drunk to start on me. I didn't get drunk. I drank a lot of alcohol while punching that bag and I actually threw punches better with drink in my stomach. The union was having a barbecue. There was around 200 people that had attended. Men woman and children had turned up and we quickly got a game of soccer going and started and played with the kids. The union boss gave a speech and thanked everyone for coming so I decided I had had enough and would walk home. I walked through the side gate and was confronted by two men. "Your the guy that has the punching bag" one said before pushing me. I always try to hit first and did. Fighting is simple if you know what your doing and trained right. When you walk into a tree branch in the dark it will knock you off your feet. The tree didn't move you walked your body through it and knocked yourself out. I always try to be like the tree branch in the dark and let them walk onto the end of my fist. You know when someone is about to hit you they tend to grit there teeth and swing back first and Its at that moment you hit them. The guy fell to ground but I let him get back up. Before I knew it he was leaning over and I was throwing uppercuts into his face. The other guy grabbed me from behind in a sleeper hold crushing my wind pipe. I

Couldn't breath and fell to the ground and luckily he let go. "we don't want any trouble "the guy that was choking me said. His mate was still unconscious and he went to his aid. I brushed myself off and walked home. The next day the SBD bosses called me into the office. At first I thought it was about the fight but it wasn't. They wanted me to go and work at another mine for 6 weeks operating machinery. I couldn't believe it as they had stopped me operating machines. I didn't want to go but they promised as soon as I was finished at Newlands Colliery I could come back. They told me to take the troop carrier with me so I could drive the men to work and also to take my punching bag. The fact that they told me to take the punching bag made me suspicious and think they would replace me when I was gone. I had no real choice if I said no they would think I let them down and it seemed my only way to get back on the machines. SBD was a great company to work for. The owner Mr Steve Bizzarca would sometimes lend blokes money that were struggling if they had to buy a car or things like that. I packed up the troop carrier and drove the 290 Klms to Glenden. The town of Glenden was built and owned by the mines. You needed there approval to be there. It had a pub, a post office and a couple of shops along with camps and houses for the miners. The mines built houses for the permanent employees and the contractors stayed in what they call dongers. Dongers are dozens of single rooms side by side built into something that looked like the back of a truck. They were demountable buildings and could be trucked and moved around easily. Even the roads were built by the mines and they rarely needed maintenance they were built that good. Once I was in town I went and found which room I was in and then I headed to the pool to swim some laps. Fitness was very important to me and the pool was built next door to the pub. The next morning I turned up for work. It seemed it was everyone's first day on the job. The SBD boss Mr Cathagy had written all of our names on a black board and he got us all to write our years of experience next to our names. There was this one guy peter that had a lot of experience but seemed to have a bad attitude straight away. It stood out as he made everyone aware he was a union member. "Ill be showering in the permanent bathroom im a union member "he said. All the permanent mine employees were all union members and they showered in a separate bathroom to the contractors. I was a union member in two states of Australia but I never told him that and I showered with the contractors because that is what we all were. Its not a good thing to let the men your working with know you think they are a scab and that is what he was doing. Scab labourers are people that work while there is a strike on. Peter was put in charge of a group of inexperienced guys and I was told to run supplies and nothing else. They also made it clear to me to only do as Dallas Wilby instructed and to not get tied up in what peter is doing. Don't pay any attention to peter was what I was instructed. That pissed peter off as Peter thought he was the boss. Dallas Wilby was our boss. Peter was the only experienced bloke working with 6 inexperienced men so they made him the leading hand. My trouble with Peter started the very first day. He wrote a report about me saying I dropped a heap roof bolts in the travelling road underground. If I did accidently drop a couple of bolts that was fine as accidents happen. Peter got in trouble for finding them and not picking them up. After that he started doing things to annoy me daily and he started arguing about who was driving the troop carrier so I let him drive to save the arguments. It didn't work. After about 5 days of this nonsense he tried to fight me underground. The bloke was huge standing about 6 feet 5 inches so I stood up to him in front of everyone he backed down. The next day he rounded up everyone a hour and a half early and drove everyone out to work leaving me behind. If that wasn't bad enough he told the boss that instead of working I was at the pub drinking and almost got me fired. I had to take the boss to the pub to check with the publican that I wasn't drinking there. The publican told the boss that I was drinking lemonade and I pointed out what was going on with Peter. They swapped me shifts so I could work with a different crew of guys. I stayed at the pub that night and did start drinking. I drank there until closing time and after it closed the publican invited me to his place to have a few drinks for his wife's birthday. At the party there was a lot of permanent miners that were union members so I told them what had been happening. I was in disbelief that all the men would turn up for work 1 and half hours early just to leave me behind and make out I was off drinking. Going over it got me wild and the union guys riled me up and told me to go sort them out. I was angry really angry as I was doing a lot of boxing and was to be sparring with a Australian champion on my days off but instead I had to work another rotation. I grabbed a 9 kilo dry chemical fire extinguisher a flogged into Peters door not realizing he wasn't in there because I was drunk. I had drank a full bottle of Sambuca before leaving the publicans house. No one came out of peters door. Thinking he was hiding inside I discharged the dry chemical fire extinguisher into the air conditioner to try and suffocate him out. I got the wrong air conditioner and suffocated the wrong bloke. The next morning I wasn't popular and awoke to a couple of punches while I was in bed sleeping. I new what was going to happen so I packed my bag to leave and headed for the food mess where I could get a ride back to Tieri. Once at Tieri I grabbed my punching bag and Hitched a ride into Rockhampton. That was the last time I ever worked in the coal mines. Broke and homeless and out of work is no place for the faint hearted as I was forced from then on to sleep in parks and homeless shelters throughout Queensland. I did file a multi million dollar lawsuit against the mining companies but was unsuccessful as it clearly was my fathers fault.

CHAPTER 13

The Enforcer

I had been living in Oznam House which is a homeless shelter for men in Rockhampton. I seemed to notice Max Gleeson everywhere I went and it turns out he was following me. "just wanted to see if you were suitable to share a house with "he said when I joked "are you following me". Max had rented a one bedroom apartment in the old cinema in Kent street but it had a little room off to the side of the bedroom. That little room was to become my new room as Max and I got acquainted over a few xxxx gold beers. Max was around 55 years old at the time and was severely scarred by his ordeals with mental health and it seemed he didn't like the term crazy. Max was a bit of a enforcer in his day known to most for driving his car into the front of a police station after they stared at him at a set of lights. There was 11 units in total all of them rented out to men with a disability and on a pension as the rent was cheap and gas and electricity included. They wouldn't rent any of the units out to girls as it caused too many fights they said. Unlike most homeless men I started every day with the gym straight after breakfast. I would box usually from 7:30am until around 9:30am and usually be the first one in the pub. I would be waiting across the road for Sue to open j jays jungle bar every day. Sue the bar lady gave us what they call bar cards on credit. Each bar card was 10 pots of beer for 17 dollars it was the cheapest beer in town. I would drink 10 pots of beer every morning then go to the homeless shelter for lunch. After lunch I would have a quick nap then drink another 10 pots before returning to the gym for another hour and a half boxing. It was safe say I could throw punches while drinking better then when sober. Being homeless can be a rough game so boxing came in handy probably saving my life once or twice. I had just finished my tenth pot and was about to head to the homeless shelter for a feed when a guy came in the bar that I knew from working in the mines. I didn't know him as in know his name but his face was really familiar and I knew the company he worked for. "Stay common stay" he pleaded when I told him I was leaving and explained I was out of money. He said his name was Greg and he offered to shout me drinks all night so I stayed. Before getting to j jays Greg had been shouting a guy drinks that was new in town and he had followed him down. Pubs are on every corner in Rockhampton and so were the hustlers if you weren't careful. The guy started trying to fight me as I was now a threat to him being shouted beers. Being a gentlemen I told him how it was first as fighting is the last thing I wanted to do as it always breaks my fingers. I told him I understood he was new in town and probably staying at the homeless shelter. I told him that I was just like him and that if he knew me a little better he wouldn't pick a fight with me. I got my mining mate to buy him a drink and that seemed to settle him down for a while. Before long Greg wanted to go see the strippers at a bar just up the road called the Savoy. I rarely drank there as it was a bit of a dive and the girls weren't that good but I agreed to go anyway. Greg forgot to shout the other guy drinks and you could tell he was blaming me. He was talking with 2 other guys at the end of the bar and they kept looking over at me. You could tell a fight was brewing. Felthouse a mate of mine had just walked in and I pulled him to the side and told him that I was worried the 3 of them would attack me. No sooner had I spoke and the 3 were headed our way. Felthouse got straight into it and was going good but the bouncer grabbed him and escorted him out as I took on the other two. I pulled one off balance as I head-butted him to the floor and quickly proceeded to land combos on the other. Kara one of the strippers jumped in to stop me and I held her out the way with my left hand which she bit pretty badly before starting to head-butt me herself. I dragged Kara through one bar door and into the other bar before heading out onto the street. It wasn't long before another guy came to Kara's rescue thinking I was fighting her so I unleashed two jabs with my right hand while letting go of Kara. When I let go of Kara her stripper clothes had came off and she was now naked. The guy I hit with jabs turned and started running but I quickly caught him up and pumped the back of his head with right hand punches knocking him out. He laid face down on the roundabout in the middle of the road. Walking backwards waiting for the guy to get up I tripped over the kerb and gutter falling to the ground. As soon as I was on the ground another guy came to kick me while I was down but as he went to walk over my feet I raised my foot into his groin. As the guys body weight came forward over my straightened leg it lifted his feet off the ground and his head came flying down onto my right hand breaking my fingers. He then crashed to the ground and didn't get up. Next minute I heard sirens and 2 police cars come flying around the corner "quick get in the toilets Demo" the publican said while he stalled them. The cops grabbed everyone else while I hid in the rest room. Back in the bar the publican gave me two ice buckets for my broken fingers and a few free beer's. We drank until closing time and then I walked Greg back to his room at Duthies Hotel. Once back at the hotel I fell asleep on one of the beds and woke up a few hours later. Greg was asleep in the bath tub so I took 60 dollars out of the pocket of his jeans and left. I could have taken several hundred but im a pretty honest sort of guy. In the morning I had to go to hospital to have my fingers fixed. The doctor treating me re broke the fingers over and over and moulded them back into shape but on the x-rays the knuckles were smashed and the fingers still give me trouble today. A few days later I came home from the pub to see Max getting wheeled out of the door by ambulance officers. Max had a knife especially sharpened by the ex butcher that lived upstairs. The knife was only to be used on tomatoes and was razor sharp. Max had ran the knife around his neck from ear to ear and the blood was sprayed across the entire kitchen floor, cupboards and walls. Its only the neighbour had came to the door by chance and seen Max laying on the floor or he'd be dead. Max spent a few weeks in a mental facility with staples in his throat that made it look like a zipper.

CHAPTER 14

In Love With The Enemy

I met Sara in 2004. She was with Scotty Boneland and I liked her looks straight away. It was one of those occasions when you see a girl and think "gee I just have to have that" and the attraction was very luring. I noticed her starting to pop up or appear everywhere I went and it wasn't long before she had me taken in with her. She seemed quite promiscuous and one time she had me pressed up against the fence while I was hanging my laundry out to dry. "has Scotty been fucking Nicole Leskie" she asked. "just tell me he has and ill fuck you now" she said. I didn't know what to say. Im quite shy when girls do things like that but never the less I wanted to have her right or wrong. I had filed a large lawsuit against the mining company Mastermyne for defamation. It got pretty messy as I drank a lot and when I got drunk I would ring there answering machine and leave messages. I had already been charged with 33 counts of phone carriage service to menace. On this particular day the Queensland State title amateur boxing tournament was on. I was supposed to fight a lad I had done some sparring with. It was early morning so I headed across to the post office hotel to have a few beers where I bumped into Scotty Boneland and Sara. While I was talking to them Scotty asked me to let him know when I was headed home as he wanted to get some weed. I drank a few beers and was going to head home so I ordered a pizza from just down the road. While waiting for the pizza I saw Scotty and Sara walking past and he had a oversize skateboard in his hand "hey Scotty "I yelled out telling him I was headed home. As I walked over to greet him he swung the skateboard at my head. I managed to move my head out of the way and had already hit him twice with my right hand jab. I jabbed twice more before hitting him with a 3 punch combo to finish him up. I actually felt sorry for him as the blood was gushing out of his lips. Once back inside the pub my brother rang my mobile phone so I walked back outside to talk with him un disturbed. He wanted to know about the boxing tournament and as we talked I heard a grunting from behind arrrrrrrrgh then crack I was hit from behind with a baseball bat by Scotty Boneland just as I turned to see it coming. I couldn't believe I was still standing and he ran away. It hurt like hell but I managed to handle the pain and stagger back inside. The whole bar had witnessed what had happened and the owner had got the bar lady to call a ambulance. When the ambulance came I said there was no baseball bat and that I slipped and fell into the power pole. I said the same thing to police who turned up shortly after the ambulance but regardless of how much I stuck to my story I don't think police believed me as they forced me to go to the hospital to have my head checked. Once at the hospital I waited until no one was looking and made my escape. If I had of stayed police would have insisted that I make a statement and I didn't want people to think that I was a police informant. I ran the 3 blocks to my place and by the time I had got there some one had tried to break in and had broken 2 louvre windows. Once inside I packed the split in my head with Vaseline to stop it bleeding then headed back to the pub to pick up my pizza. I didn't fight at the boxing tournament for obvious reasons I drank beer instead until closing time. It wasn't long before Sara was on my door step. She said she had caught Scotty with Nicky Leskie and they were having sex under the house. She stuck to me like glue from that moment on. I didn't mind as I had been on my own for years. It was about 4 weeks later and I was in bed when Sara got up to go to the toilet. It was about 1am in the morning and when she came back I noticed she didn't shut the door. I've always had a bit of a sixth sense and I Sensed something was wrong. I grabbed a baseball bat and headed out the door where I was immediately approached by a guy wielding a knife. The guy stabbed me in the throat so I hit him with the bat but only got him in the shoulder. "quick get him "he yelled out alerting me that there was more. I turned and put my back against the fence so no one could come from behind and I saw there was only 2 of them. Max slid his door open and turned on the light so I quickly rushed between the two then turned around hitting the first one to approach me until he fell down. The remaining guy didn't seem to want to tackle me on his own so I dragged the one that I hit inside so I could find out who he was. It didn't take long and rumours started to spread that the mining company had taken a hit out on me. Scotty Boneland was driving around in a Trans-am worth around $20,000 in 2004 and no one could seem to explain where he got the money. Fearing the worst I grabbed Sara and bought bus tickets to forster a town north of Sydney where my parents lived. My neck was still bleeding days later as I never went to hospital again worried people would think I was a informant. Once at my parents place my father closed the wound with butterfly style Band-Aids. Although my parents helped us they didn't really want us there as they were frightened of me because of there involvement in the lawsuit I had against Mastermyne. My father asked when we were leaving as soon as he picked us up from the bus. In the hurry we had forgotten one important thing we forgot Maisy Sara's 4 year old daughter as she lived with Sara's mum. I was sleeping on the lounge and Sara was slumped over my face and I felt the tears. "we forgot Maisy "she said. Happy to get rid of us my father bought a cheap station wagon to drive back and get her. He also bought us a 12 man tent again indicating he didn't want us at his place on our return. The drive was long but we made it back to Rockhampton after staying at Sara's grandmothers place in Brisbane. Once in Rockhampton Sara's mother was reluctant to let us leave for a camping trip with the 4 year old but I just packed up everything including the pet rat and we went. We drove back to N.S.W to a town called Taree. We went to Taree as it was Christmas time and most of the caravan parks near the ocean were booked out. We also had to be close to pick up the methadone we took daily as both Sara and I had become addicted to morphine.

Camping was a breeze but eventually the rain would come and come it did so my father bought us a caravan. Sara was very promiscuous and at times she would leave me and Maisy asleep in the car. She would go to the shop to get milk and end up seeing a job cleaning a motel. She would then go and flirt with the motel owner. I had to keep my eye on her more then the 4 year old as stranger danger really concerned me. After 3 months holidaying Sara and I decided to take Maisy home to Rockhampton. The plan was Sara and Maisy would catch a train and I would wait for Sara to return. We were going to spend one month holidaying on our own but once Sara was in Rockhampton it was very hard to get her to return. Eventually I had to catch a plane and go and fetch her. I missed her badly and couldn't wait to hold her when she picked me up at Rockhampton Airport. We only stayed in Rockhampton for a few days then caught a coach back to N.S.W. The coach had a stop over in Brisbane so Sara and I headed up Brisbane's red light district to score some drugs and have a look around. We ended up going into a strip club after taking drugs. Sara and I got talking with the owner of the club about the possibility of Sara becoming a stripper so he showed us around the place. He went over the amounts of money and what was expected of the girls in return. To my surprise Sara wanted to have a go there and then but I wouldn't let her. I wouldn't stop her normally its just we were out of time. Once back on the bus we sat right up the back where there were plenty of empty seats and had sex. Along with increased sexual appetite amphetamines can make you delusional and paranoid. Pretty soon after the sex Sara and I were experiencing delusions and started getting paranoid of each other. I cant remember the exact details but we started fighting a few hours before we were due to arrive in Taree. We sat apart as we didn't want to disturb anyone and once off the bus we started fighting again. My parents were there to pick us up and they became frightened of me and Sara fighting and got the service station attendant to call police. The police arrested me stopping me from being able to pick up my methadone. If you don't take the methadone every day you get very sick and as it was I was going to try sneak half of my dose and give it to Sara as she had been cut off the program when she went to Queensland. My parents and police decided to separate Sara and I and they put Sara on a train back to Queensland while they held me in custody. Angry I went to the toilet all over the floor and threw it everywhere. They had no right to have me there as I hadn't broken the law. Eventually after Sara's train had departed they let me go but they had put a apprehended violence order between me and my parents stating I was to have no contact with them. It was a breach or abuse of police powers as I hadn't done anything. I had no money and had to bribe a taxi driver to drive me the 20 kilometres to my car and caravan then swap the taxi driver my punching bag for the fare. I now had to wait 3 days to go to court and I was forced to have to drive without a license to get my methadone each day as Sara was usually the driver. I was really worried about Sara as she had no money and had to get off the train in Brisbane. She had to get off near the strip club we went to and I thought she may see that as a way to get money and drugs. When the matter finally went to court I represented myself. I pointed out to the judge that my parents fear of me was brought about there involvement in the Defamation lawsuit I had with Mastermyne and I handed him a copy. I asked for a stay in proceedings until the outcome of the lawsuit which he granted as the law is very clear that if persons involved in criminal court actions are also involved in a defamation action the defamation action must come first. The lawyer I had draft my lawsuit against Mastermyne made sure I was well read about the defamation laws and the judge was very angry at the police for what they had done. Sara had no mobile phone all I could do is wait and hope to hear from her which never happened until 5 days later. When she rang Sara simply said "are you coming or not "so I packed up the van and got a refund on the rent I had paid in advance. I drove straight through driving most of the 2000 kilometres in one go accept for a little stop in Brisbane trying to get heroin and one stop where I grabbed 2 hours sleep. Driving down the inner city streets through Brisbane to where I knew I could get heroin was challenging given I was towing a caravan. Eventually I found a place I could park and get out of the car. I picked up a prostitute that said she could get the heroin across town. She got me to wait at a park telling me there was a few overdoses just the other day and pointing out the police taped sections. The overdoses was a good sign and meant the heroin was really pure if it was killing people. A few minutes went past and then I was confronted by a heap of police officers and detectives wanting to search my van. I said they could no problem as at that stage I had nothing to hide. It seemed they thought I was transporting heroin as it was very uncommon to see a car towing a caravan right in the middle of the city where people were known to sell and use drugs. The prostitute never came back. I don't know if she got busted or was just worried about police hanging around. I drove straight out of town onto the Bruce highway. The Bruce highway ran all the way to Rockhampton. I was so relieved to get out of the city traffic after being on the road for about 14 hours straight. After about 19 hours driving I had to take a break and pulled up at a Matilda road house and hopped in the van and grabbed a couple hours sleep. Whilst asleep someone must have syphoned my tank as it was a very old ford and easy to do. The reason I think it was syphoned was I ran out of petrol about one hour away from Rockhampton and the petrol gauge said I still had half a tank. As soon I heard and felt the car run out of petrol I rolled as far as I could trying to find a safe place to pull off the edge of the road. I only had about 15 seconds of rolling before the car stopped in the middle of the road. I had no choice but to put two wheels and one side of the van off the road on a embankment that was a 45 degrees angle and I was lucky I didn't roll over. It was pitch black darkness but I could hear the whirring sound of a car coming in the distance so I immediately put on the right hand blinker and got out of the car In case it got hit. I raced past the back of the caravan so I could get completely off the road. As the car approached it slowed down and came to a complete stop. It was hard to make out what sort of car it was in the dark. "What's up mate "the passenger said after rolling down his window. I told him I ran out of petrol. "Where ya going to" he asked saying hed give me a lift into town. I had to think quick as everything I possessed in the world was inside that car and caravan. Would it be safe I thought. I asked if they had a phone I could use to ring Sara to come get me somehow so I could stay with our things. The driver said he had a car phone and if I was going to use it it would probably better I jumped in the car. "Wow what sort of car is this" I asked as I opened up the back door. BMW the driver said but not a ordinary BMW it was $200,000 worth. Car phones weren't common in 2004 unless it was in a luxury car. Sara couldn't come until the morning as it was 2am and her mother wouldn't let her. They were actually angry that I rang so late and it seems they didn't appreciate the situation. If I stayed It wouldn't be safe to sleep in the van as it could get hit by a truck so I decided to lock the car and go with the two in the BMW. The guy in the passenger seat offered me a joint as soon as we started driving but I don't smoke weed. Weed is like kryptonite to me it makes me scared and weak. "No thanks" was my response "but you do as you wish" I told him after he went to put it out. Sitting in the back was like sitting on a private jet it sure was a beautiful car. The two were headed past Airlie beach. It didn't take long and the guys were trying to persuade me into running prostitutes for them but I said no to that as well. I was so relieved to see Sara when the BMW dropped me off. I had to apologize for my parents putting her on a train and only giving her $20. The next morning Sara and I borrowed her mums car and took a can of petrol out to the caravan. Thankfully no one had touched it. When we got back to Sara's parents with the van it seems they already had a spot picked out for the van to go. It was a good spot hidden by the house but one side had to be elevated on bricks. I don't think the mother liked me too much. She did like me but we had a argument at Christmas before we left and it wasn't long before she was up my nose again. I cant remember the details all I remember is packing up the van to leave and she had called the cops to say I was driving without a license. Police were waiting up the road but as I was about to drive out of the drive way Sara took over. Once the van was secure at my brother's place I went to see Baxter's real-estate to rent a house. Baxter's were great offering me my old unit back or if Sara and Maisy were going to be with me they had a nice 3 bedroom place for us. I asked Sara which should it be and she told me to take the 3 bedroom place. I quickly renewed acquaintances with old friends and started to do a little business with the weed. During the day Sara was out near her mums. She was bored so I used to let her drive one of my drug dealing mates around while he dropped off drugs. That would be my down fall as he ended up fucking her. I didn't mind its just the fact that they lied about it at first. The housing commission ended up getting Sara a duplex house on the other side of town and she had just agreed to have me moving in with her instead of keeping the two houses and paying rent for them both. I hadn't moved in with her just yet when She wasn't where she was supposed to be. I went looking for her and I checked to see if she had picked Maisy up from school and she hadn't so I drove to her place with my brother looking for her. The guy next door came out with a axe saying "I heard what you've been doing to the young lady" he obviously had made a mistake but he came at me with the axe so I picked up half a brick that was in the garden and threw it at him. The brick missed him and went straight through Sara's front window. I never found Sara I went home and was arrested by police. Police put a DVO between Sara and I saying I couldn't see her. The matter had to go to court the next day. I turned up for court and was in the library part of the courthouse for a short while. When I went into the actual courtroom they told me that my matter had been dealt with without me. The court had set full orders for 2 years that I have no contact with Sara and Maisy. The court Magistrate wasn't allowed to do that all she could do is set the matter down for a hearing and set a temporary order but the application made by police didn't seek any temporary orders. The matter would go on to cause a lot of problems and on occasions be the subject of appeal. In Sara's statement it said that Sara and I were never in a relationship. It said she met me up the mental health and found out I mowed lawns and allowed me to mow hers. The statement said that I had become more and more obsessed with Sara and they caught me looking through there windows while they were getting dressed. I don't know to this day if Sara said those things or if police made them up but I would end up in prison 9 times because of the DVO and 5 times because of Sara.

CHAPTER 15

Burn Baby Burn

We still had the old Ford Falcon station wagon my father bought for Sara and I. It was a very good old car but Sara gave it a rough time. She had slammed up the back of a car deliberately while we fighting one time and I had to change the bonnet. She also had trouble getting it in my drive way without scraping the sides on my gate. She got frustrated easy and I remember breaking my ribs diving off the stairwell through the passenger window and jamming the automatic gear shift back into park. She was arguing with me and had jumped in the car and held the accelerator flat to the floor while she jammed it into gear. I only just caught it in time or she would have taken out my fence. I think I loved that car and she knew it so she destroyed it deliberately but I just kept fixing it. As I said before during the day I was letting her take the car and drive Smithy around while he dropped off drugs. I did that to keep her occupied plus it kept her out of my way while I organized my on business but she ended up fucking him so I suggested she stay with him and I let them use the car. I had struck up a relationship with a beautiful girl named ebony but I used to share her with 6ft 5 guy named Red. He text her one time while she was with me asking her out so I invited him over and just told him straight we could share her and for a while it worked. Nicol Leskie had been found raped and murdered and it was later revealed that Red helped move the body. Sara hated Nicol because she fucked scotty boneland while she was with him. The guy that killed Nicol was named Steven and I bumped into him at the pub before he had been caught. "I've been looking for you everywhere" he said when he seen me. I don't know why as I didn't know him that well but he tried to explain. He was saying that there was a job on offer a really big job and that no one could step up and take it accept him. At the time he left me confused but after some things im about to reveal it could be taken that Nicol's death was a paid hit. I believe Nicol Leskie's grandfather was one of the Melbourne gangland figures and I know she was known to Jason Moran and family or at least that's what she told me. I believe its true because I had a centre page double page liftout of all the Melbourne gangland figures and a old guy named Leskie was one of them. However it may of had nothing to do with that but it could have been revenge. The second person Steven killed was Ed Payne and Ed Payne's father was one of the Melbourne gangsters. Perhaps Nicol's death had something to do with me as there was a rumour there was a hit on my head and im left wondering was it a attempt to frame me. When they found Nicol dead my car was searched by police but not for drugs. The police went all through the carpet with tweezers from what Sara told me like it was searched by forensics and I remember one time when Sara brought the car back I found a set of girls clothing and Doc Martins jammed under the seat. Some friends said they were Nicol's and Nicole used to wear Doc Martins and a leather jacket the same as the one I found. After police searched it it came back with the carpet from the back of the wagon torn out and the funny thing is I never wanted the car back it was like they were forcing it on me. One other time Sara came and got it only to pour petrol all through it and burn it down Lakes Creek Road. After she burnt it she told police that I did it and they tried as hard as they could to charge me but I was with people in a pub at the time. I would later find out that Red helped move Nicol's body and it was known to me that Red took Sara out the bush and put a gun in her mouth and threatened her to never talk about something. Perhaps they used my car to move the body. When police found Nicol dead they dragged in 52 people and for me that is a hell of a lot of people to be questioned over a murder and it seems there's a lot more involved then we have been led to believe. Some even knew what was going to happen to Nicol and I wonder why didn't they stop Steven from killing. Red almost shot me over something one time when I got out of prison. I responded to some text messages on my phone from who I thought was ebony. The messages were inviting me to Reds place saying she was under his house almost naked and swimming in a baby's pool. I drove around there with a guy I didn't really know I had just met him at a girls place. He wanted to come so I took him. When we pulled up at Reds I told the guy to wait in the car while I asked Red if it was ok. Red let me in the door "just go on through to the kitchen we can talk about it there" he said. After I walked into the kitchen I turn around to a shotgun pointed at me" what have you done cunt" he said before butt slapping me over and over. I told him I didn't know what he was talking about. After he butt slapped me about 6 times the butt snapped off the shotgun and as it did I ran to the front door and made my escape but my bag containing my phone got left behind. When I jumped in the car the guy was gone and as I drove away I noticed all four tyres had been let down. I drove on the rims for about a kilometre and a half to the Lakes Creek Tavern and pulled in there to have a beer. Blood was gushing out of my head and although the publican poured me a beer he called police. I don't know if I told him what had happened, perhaps I did and that's why he called them. Police said they had a care of duty and couldn't let me go in that state without taking me to the hospital and tricked me. They took me to the police station not to the hospital trying to get me to make a statement instead. I wouldn't talk but I was going to its just they kept pissing me off with the way they were treating me and eventually they let me leave. I went back a day later with a baseball bat. I got a friend named Ricky to drive me. He must have saw me getting out of the car and as I approached his staircase he came running down at me. I ran as fast as I could up the road and every time he stopped I turned around to hit him. We did that same routine about 4 times and each time he stopped I hit him in the shoulder. Eventually he dove into my stomach grabbing me around the waist and tackling me to the ground. I had him in a headlock and I pulled tight as hard as I possibly could to cut off his airway. Laying flat on my back he walked his hands all over my face searching for my eyes which he eventually found. I didn't know it at the time but he pushed his finger straight through my left eye lid as he eye gouged me in both eyes. The feeling was unbearable as he wiggled his fingers back and forth so I squeezed his neck even harder mustering every bit of strength I had until he started having convulsions but his fingers were still in my eyes. This went on for a few minutes and I was almost exhausted when I heard Ebony saying to let him go "let him go Demo" she was saying while she banged the baseball bat beside my head. I let him go and his fingers came out of my eyes. I couldn't see I was completely blinded all I could do was lay there. He got to his feet and stomped on my head a couple of times and took off. All I could do was yell out for Ricky until his car pulled up beside me. I felt my way up his car door and found the door handle and got in. My eye sight slowly creeped back and there was blood all over me as the cuts from 2 days beforehand had come open. I got Ricky to take me to a friends house so I could clean myself up but blood persisted to run from the hole in my eye lid for a few days. A couple of days had passed and I received a phone call from Ebony wanting me to pick her up from Reds. I didn't know if it was a setup so I went in taxi cab instead. When we pulled up Ebony was waiting on the stairwell but wouldn't come down. I opened the door and started getting out when Red came running out from under the house. I fell back into the seat and screamed at the taxi driver to go as Red had a steel bar in his hands. The taxi driver flattened it and took off but then hit the brakes shortly after and Red almost got me through the window. The taxi driver took off and then stopped a couple of times until I said to go up the end of the road. "now what "the taxi driver asked so I told him to turn around and drive toward Red and he did. As we approached him I told him to drive my side of the car as close to him as he could. I opened the door to hit him but missed as the driver swerved then hit the bakes shortly after. I looked around and Red was running towards the back of the car so I told the driver to go and as he did Red has thrown the steel bar and it hit the back of the car. The taxi driver then drove about 500 metres up the road and stopped saying he wasn't moving any further and calling the police. There was a shop across the road so I got them to call me another taxi and luckily the taxi got there before the police did. A few days later a friend of Reds gave me my bag back.

CHAPTER 16

Unsolved

The year was approximately 2012 and I was selling everything, weed speed ice ecstasy and morphine along with the occasional ounce of heroin however we had only just started with heroine you didnt come across it much in Rockhampton. We had some new Asian counter parts that seemed to have plenty of it and in all different grades of purity. As I said you never seen heroin much in Rockhampton but they sold lots of morphine. We wanted to try the heroin as the morphine crowd were a tricky bunch for me. When I would get the morphine organized and nice and reliable a bloke called nipper would somehow fuck it up for me. Nipper was fucking my ex Sara and he had become obsessed in causing me trouble. Nipper was never happy in his relationship unless I was in prison where he was sure I couldn't root his girlfriend. I never fucked her but he was clearly sick with thinking I was. He was one of my mates I had taken over a lot of drug business he used to do but I found a way to keep him happy. I told him to buy 2 ounces of ice from us every time we bought a pound and hold it. There will be days I would run out and would need it during the time it took to get more. "I'll buy them off you" I told him and for more then what he paid" Why would you do that" he asked and I told him simply so I don't ever have to say no to anyone. If you say no it means you ran out and a sign that they need someone else to buy from. I didn't want anyone else to be able to find the opportunity to start up competition. It was our town for a while and I wanted to keep it that way and besides if people know you've run out then they know you are picking up and could tell police. I remember the day I took Sara around Nippers house and left her in the car. He went off his head "why bring that dog to my place" he said. He hated her guts as she was a bad police informant but usually only told police about me. Sara had me put in prison shortly after meeting nipper it was a complete setup with her and the cops and of course Sara went witness against me. While I was in prison Sara thinking I got the pounds of ice from nipper turned on the charm for him. She turns up there and gets straight on his cock in 5 seconds. Of course I didn't know until months later when I got out of prison. He wrote a letter saying he had my car and things. In the letter he knew I was going for supreme court bail in a few days. He would have known because police would advise the witness that I had applied for bail meaning he had contact with Sara. Nipper wrote to turn up in the afternoon if I was successful with my bail and grab my car and things. I got bail but the prison wouldn't let me go until about 4:20pm with just enough time to make it to Centrelink. There was a domestic violence order between Sara and I and I couldn't go within 100 metres of her. What he did was hide her in his bedroom while I was there. He did this deliberately to set me up. He invited me inside and he actually told me that he had been fucking my Mrs and I said "that's awesome it will keep her out of my pockets and into yours "meaning his wallet. She ran out and smashed a coffee mug over my head and I immediately took off from there. Nipper called police straight away and within 20 minutes I was back in custody. I was howling mad and very angry as I just did 4 and half months in prison and was only out a few hours. Now it would be several more months before I was free again. Whilst a free man Nipper would constantly fight with Sara thinking I was fucking her. I hardly saw Sara and when I did see her it was obvious she had come deliberately to set me up for police. I wasn't allowed any contact with her so she would find me and just hop into my car. Other times she would find a bar I was at and go into the other bar and call police. She would say she was there and that I had turned up looking for her. She was the baddest police informant I have ever come across in my life. I can't believe she is alive today as my colleagues wanted her dead bad. She costs us hundreds of thousands of dollars in lost drug money. Every time I got arrested all the drug movement we were doing would get shut down as I had some of the boys hold the drugs and another hold the money my head was already on show so I pretended I had all the drugs with me while I sold it. The shut down would cost us millions as we did about $100,000 worth every ten days since 2005. This particular time Nipper and Sara were fighting and had split up. That meant to Sara and Nipper that I had go to prison because unless I was in prison they couldn't be happy. Nipper had text me telling me he had finished with Sara. They dead set stalked the absolute fuck out of me week in and week out and when he would ring I would have to answer to him or he will talk Sara into finding me and calling police. Straight away I was thinking here we go its prison time again. maybe today I would think, maybe tonight I just knew it wouldn't be long. Nipper told me time and time again the same rubbish and that he wanted Sara to spend some time with me. I would say "no thanks". I would say no. Sara blames him for keeping her away from me. To her I was her best friend it was sickening stuff and yes they are both mental health patients. This day Nipper tells me he is with another Sarah a totally different girl and that Sarah and Sara were on they're way to my house wanting a shot of heroin. I actually agreed and told him that I would give both of them a shot. I had no choice if I say fuck off they'll just find another way to bait me up. When the girls got there I had changed my mind and I wasn't going to give this Sarah anything at all. I told her I only had enough for Sara. I sent her away and About 30 minutes later Nipper rings. He starts saying I was going away for a life time this time so him and Sara could live together in peace. He said he had dosed up Sarah's coffee but it was my heroin they were going to find. Within a few hours I had found out Sarah was dead and Nipper was saying I killed her. I actually can't remember if he went straight to police or he jus told doctors all about it. He told doctors so they would go to the police. Doctors are bound buy law to go to the police if someone makes allegations like that. To cut a long story short he kept making appointments at community health doctor's every few days. he would tell them that I injected Sarah with heroin and killed her so they had to tell police and do a proper autopsy or they would assume I would get away with murder if it was me. Trouble he had with this tactic was it was already old as he had been doing it over and over. They got files from his other doctors and all the records were about was me selling drugs and stuff. He didn't want people to think he was a police informant so he used doctors to call police for him. Community health did another autopsy and proved that he was lying as it was a Xanax overdose. for 6 months he kept meeting with heaps of doctors and counsellors. He met with police telling them how I overdosed her with heroin. Community health workers came to see me about Nipper trying to frame me. They were really concerned about him being obsessed as he had made dozens of appointments in which all he did was talk lies about me they said and his story's kept changing all the time. I confirmed he had been doing it for about 3 to 4 years non stop. I couldn't kill him police would know straight away it was me. if someone killed him or he overdosed police would sniff around and the police were just as bad as these people as far as I was concerned. They were busted over and over writing false statements. She was found dead with him not me and he lied about it and yes it was his Xanax that was in her system as he was prescribed. He put it in her coffee as he told me on the phone thinking he was smart. I wouldn't talk to the police about anything. I shouldn't have to it's obvious as he was prescribed Xanax and he lived with her and he sent Sarah to my place to get a shot of heroin. When I found out she was living with him I told her to fuck off at the door, grabbed the other Sara, my Sara and gave her a shot. I think what gave Nipper the idea was my Sara used to overdose all the time and I've been locked up for saving her life Because of the Domestic violence order. I would turn up at the house and give her CPR after talking with her on the phone as she dropped dead. I plead compulsion and duress and was found not guilty but they caused me a lot of hours in custody over it and a court battle to get myself out again. Compulsion and Duress under section 31 of the criminal code says its not against the law to break the law to up hold the law from being broken or to save someone from injury or death but it has to be proportionate and equal to the circumstances. I represented myself in court 95% of the time and the 5% of the times I used a solicitor they failed to get me free. My boys wanted Sara murdered but I said no. She and Nipper put me in prison 13 times in about 7 years sometimes for 5 weeks sometimes 7 months. For months I was accused of Sarah's murder and she was murdered I'm sure of that. These people tried this 3 times in Rockhampton but I never complained I just proved I didn't do it. You would assume police would charge the two people that used to be with these people when they were found dead. it was proven they lied and tried to say that I administered the fatal injection what more do they need. On another occasion phone records showed text messages from them saying they had money they owed me and to hurry up and come over. When I got there a bloke called Damien was dead on the floor so I called the ambulance. The ambulance came and picked up the body. Sara said he overdosed after I gave him a shot about 20 minutes before the ambulance got there. The body stunk he had been dead for at least 20 hours and I couldn't stay inside the smell was that bad. The fact he was dead for 20 hours is what got me off from being charged. Both witnesses said I had only been there 20 minutes and injected him straight away. Even after I gave the speech at Damien's funeral Sara and Nipper insisted that I killed him and that's what everyone thinks happened. Friends tell me "you'll get caught for it Demo" but the truth doesn't bend and there story's always do. There's one more murder where she did the exact same thing but did not know I was in police custody. She injected my flat mate at around 11:45 am in the morning with pure meth that was just cooked. It was dropped off for me whilst I wasn't there. 56 100mg morphine tablets were supposed to be with Debbie my little Irish flatmate. I know that meth was given to her because police told me 3days after having me in custody for murder. They said that she died of a amphetamine over dose and that's unheard of. Anyway police let me out of custody the day she died about 5pm that afternoon. In the morning just before police arrested me I dropped Irish at her doctor's appointment at 10am to get the 56 100ml capanol morphine tabs. $5600 that would fetch me in two days work not bad for a $5.60 script. I had the keys to the unit and cops had me in custody at 10:20am. She got home around 11am the chick that was driving us said and She was locked out of the unit but that was ok. I had put a bed in a room that No one knew we had that was adjacent to our unit. it was supposed to be our laundry but I would rest guys in there that were holding drugs for me. At some stage the cook has turned up to drop of my share of the cook. The cook and his girlfriend were hopeless morphine junkies and couldn't ever fund the equipment and chemicals to be able to cook. I had the money side of things covered. Not being able to resist the cook has swapped 17 morphine tablets for pure meth and that is actually quite a lot for a little 52 year old lady to have its enough to kill her 3 times over. When I got home I was really mean to Irish as I busted her red handed writing a affidavit against me for Nipper to give to police. I can't remember how I let her inside the unit or where I originally found her. I just remember she had ash from the astray in her mouth. I couldn't understand anything she said except for I love you demo as I put her In the ambulance. Witnesses said they had seen her violently I'll since 12 o'clock and Sara was there all day. You would think Sara or one of the witnesses would have called a ambulance for her. Police held me in custody through two coronial inquiries but it wasn't too bad I was used to it. When I said I was mean I Had called her a dog a few times in front of people and that's why they thought I killed her. I've been through a lot so nothing fazes me too much and I thought she was acting and pretending she was sick. As soon as I got her inside I had to take care of drug business as people were hounding me and it was about a hour before I called the ambulance. She died some time later in the hospital. Shortly after I put Irish in the ambulance Sara rang saying to come to her place as she wanted to buy some morphine she said. Once at her place I needed to go to the toilet so I did. My phones never stopped ringing and I needed to use my hands so I sat down to pee. I could hear Sara talking to someone but it wasn't clear who it was and pretty soon after that police came and arrested me. They never told me Irish had died until 3 days later whilst in the courtroom, the judge told me. I guess police wanted to see if I new she was dead before they told me and they allowed me several phone calls. They questioned me and asked me to recite the last 24 hours so I went one better and told them the last 48 hours. After they released me I still had to pick up the drugs as I had paid for my share in advance. I was now also rendered homeless as the unit we lived in was now a crime scene so I went and stayed at the homeless shelter on Alma street. The cook was always hard to get a hold of on the phone. After he cooked all he did was have sex and a lot of people had turned there back on me over the murder. It was 12 midnight and I was arguing in text messages with a bloke called Veechi. Veechi had kept on threatening me that he would kill me so of course I would threaten him back. The texts of threats were going back and forth and right in the middle of it the cook text. I didn't know it was the cook I thought it was Veechi I was texting and I threatened the cook by mistake. Next thing I get threats from the cook and I thought what a hide he had as it was him that owed me. I threatened him that I would wrap a blanket around myself and jump straight through his lounge room window and it was on. Knowing me the cook knew I was serious and it was likely I would see the threats through so he set out to get me first. 2 days had past and I was in a car with a heap of boys near the Sun City Tennis Club. We came around the corner and drove past the cook coming the other way. We were going to turn around but a police car came down the road so we cut across a couple of streets "what do we do the driver asked" so I got him to park into someone's driveway out of sight in case the police came looking. When we felt the coast was clear we doubled back looking for the cook and spotted his van obviously looking for us. I told the driver to go park at the Sun City Tennis Club and told them to go inside and not get involved "ill handle this" I told them. No sooner had we pulled up and the cook drove in the car park. 2 guys and a chick along with cook got out and they were all wielding baseball bats. Baseball bats actually aren't that good as you just let them swing and miss and hit them after the bat goes past before they can re-load for another swing. The cook came at me with the bat and I hit him when he missed. My hand got caught up in my bum bag that was slung over my shoulder and it caused me to miss the second punch and the bag got snapped lose in the scuffle. I danced and ducked all around the car park striking punches at the cook with every swing he took but I was moving away most of the time so there was times I was moving backwards and I tripped over a sign. I was now laying flat on my back and the cook seized the opportunity and started swinging fully loaded swings at my head. I had no choice but to put my arm up and it was broken pretty bad as he swung about 9 times into it. I was screaming for him to stop but he kept on swinging grunting as he swung. I somehow managed to climb up to my feet while blocking the bat with my broken arm and he got about 3 hits into my leg and hip snapping that as well as my leg wouldn't work. I've never thought it possible to run on one leg but that's almost what I did as I hopped really fast away from him. I think he was almost out of energy as he didn't seem to pursue me very much. I hopped straight inside the club and the manager said "im calling the police" as he saw what had happened. I actually hung up the phone as he was trying to ring and told him it wasn't necessary. The cook took off grabbing my bum bag as they went which had my wallet full of money and my phone. I couldn't stay standing so I got down on the ground and rocked side to side trying to soak up the pain. I must have looked like squashed ant would after a person walked on it. I got the driver to go to the cooks house and get the bum bag back. He picked me up about 15 minutes later and I was still in agony so they dumped me off at a friends house and rounded all the Methadone Tamazapam and Valium they could to ease my pain. I swallowed a heap of pills and drank some Methadone and went to sleep and when I woke I ate and drank and swallowed some more pills. I slept continuously for 6 days and after that I was ok but I missed my lawsuit decision going to court. Perhaps it was deliberate.

CHAPTER 17

Inside Information

Nipper was always a bit of a sly dog. Before the murders I was staying with a woman named Leanne and we lived over near the Rockhampton hospital. She would often drive my car while I dropped off drugs as I didn't have a license. She wouldn't do it for free though I was always having to spoon feed her with drugs. Sometimes drug addicts will do anything for a fix. It was a day the same as any day and I was waiting on 6 ounces of ice and speed to be dropped off. Because of the arrangement I had with Nipper he knew what I had coming. He was waiting on a ounce or 2 which he would buy from me and hang onto until I ran out. I had taken a heap of Morphine to help me relax as I hardly ever slept and when I did it would only be for a hour or two. Because I sold weed, speed, ice and morphine my phone would ring every minute of the day until about 3am. At 3am every night it would go quiet and I would get 3hours time to myself. The weed smokers would want there breakfast bongs and start ringing from 6am so I barely slept and I usually just lay on my back with both my phones sitting on my chest. I couldn't afford to sleep as people would try and take my stuff which I would hide in my pillow case or down my pants. Tired from the morphine I sat in Leanne's kitchen at the table and nodded off. When I had arrived home Nipper and a guy called Steve were in the house talking to Leanne but they left straight away when I returned. At the time I didn't think anything of it but while I was resting they kept ringing up Leanne and talking to her. I must of sat there for about 2 hours when all of a sudden there was a lot of yelling with some guy saying "where is he". Next minute 2 guys wielding baseball bats came into the kitchen and started demanding the drugs and punching me over and over in the face. "where is it" the guy would say before hitting me again. I told him I didn't have anything but they wouldn't believe me and just kept hitting me it was really frightening as I had no drugs to give them to make them stop. I had a hammer sitting on the table just in case something like this happened but it happened so quick they were able to move the hammer out of my reach. "Hang on fuck ya" I said calling out to Leanne to get my bag. Inside the bag I had specially made cans with screw on tops that I hid the drugs in. I got the cans out of my bag and showed them they were empty and I told them they were too early. Had they been a hour later I would of had the drugs so I told them that. They now were going to kidnap me so I told them to rob the person I get it from saying if they have 6 ounces to give me imagine how much they would have. After all it wasn't just me that they gave it to. They decided not to take me and said that if I was serious to let them know and they gave me a phone number. After they left I went and got a hamburger as I was hungry but now I wish hadn't as I had deep cuts inside my cheeks and eating seemed to make them worse. The Drugs came but the boys only gave me one ounce instead of 6 just in case. The next day while I was sitting out the front a car pulled up and a guy got out. It was the same guy from the night before "relax "he said im not here for trouble. He said his name was Roy and he apologized for what had happened saying it could have been avoided had the others involved got the timing right. All they had to do was ring when the drugs were there and maybe I wouldn't have been hit so much he said. He got me thinking and I realized that Nipper had set me up and even Leanne was involved. Turns out Roy was a known standover man and he had done about 9 years in prison for the same thing. He let me know he was really angry about there failure saying he would sort them out. A few days later I went to Nippers as I never let him know that I knew he was involved. Nipper was having trouble moving around and he complained about his stomach. After a while he showed me the bruises and it looked like he had bin kicked by a horse. When I asked him what had happened he said a bloke robbed him and hit him in the stomach with a pick handle. Of course when I said they could rob the person I got it from I was only saying that to make them stop hitting me im very loyal. Roy would ring every now and then telling me he had a shotgun and laughing but I never saw him again. The only time I ever got robbed was by a aboriginal guy. He rang wanting a 8 ball and at the time I was selling them for $550. A 8ball is 3.5 grams 1/8 one eight of a ounce. I was in the back of a friends car and he handed me one $50 note wrapped around a heap of $5 notes. He simply said where's the gear and quickly flashed the money as if he was handing it to me and he grabbed the bag out of my hand and ran.

CHAPTER 18

Three Is A Charm

I was living in a Anglicare housing unit in Burnett street Rockhampton. There were 8 units out the front and 8 out the back and the trouble was constant ever since I moved there. They had moved in a heap of us white fellas and black fellas together which was a recipe for disaster. I lived in the unit upstairs of the front block of units. Ashley frequently drank downstairs in the unit directly below me and at the time I didn't know him. He had been in the paper and on the news for stealing a salt water crocodile from the Rockhampton Zoo that was all I knew about him. I was in a very hyped up mood and telling a story to a few mates when I heard a knock on my door "what" I said after opening the door "what do you want". It was Ashley and a few other guys in the stairwell and no sooner had I opened the door he ran away. Sometimes when the guys would drink down stairs they would get drunk and want to fight me and im guessing that that's what had happened. A couple of weeks later and my friend David was having his hair bleached whilst sitting on my lounge. Patsy his girlfriend was standing up massaging bleach into his hair. No sooner had she sat down and bang! A huge rock came through the window and hit the wall. Because things like this were common at those units Anglicare had told me if anyone does any damage to ring the police. They said I didn't have tell on anyone just say I didn't see who did it so it was covered by insurance so that's what I did. Im sure it was Ashley but police arrested a 14 year old boy in the laneway beside the units. It would have had to be a grown man to throw a rock that size and do the damage it did to the wall. It was about 2am and I was laying on my bed when I heard a knock at the door. I looked through the peep hole and saw Ashley so I immediately opened the door. Ashley took one step inside and held a apple knife into the right side of my throat. He was saying I called police on him and that they turned up at his place. "no they didn't" I said telling him he was full of it. Next thing he started hacking into my forehead with a razor blade knife in his other hand. I punched him once with my right hand and he fell against the door of unit directly across from me. Grabbing him by the jumper I lifted him up and threw him as hard as I could down the staircase but as I did he came to and grabbed hold of me. Whether I liked it or not we both were going over the staircase and I wobbled at the top for a moment trying to balance and resist falling over. Everything was happening in slow motion so I grabbed him and jumped to try and make a better landing for myself but I hit the wall head first. I hit that hard It took everything I could muster to stay conscious. Ashley laid crumpled up unconscious at the bottom of the stairwell so I jumped on his head and ran up the stairs and shut the door. Before long police were knocking so I opened up the door and let them in. I had been sitting on the lounge with paper towel trying to stop the bleeding. "we'll have take you to the hospital" the police said. At the hospital I found out that a security guard had spotted Ashley and another guy getting out of a taxi with cricket bats and the two started fighting and he called police. Ashley and the other guy had a friend who was a taxi driver and it must have been him driving. Ashley plead guilty to unlawful wounding and spent almost 2 years behind bars. When Ashley stole the crocodile they didn't tape it up properly and it clawed them in the car when they were trying to get away with it. They pulled over and got out and the crocodile got away and was never seen again. They have photographed a saltwater crocodile in a town south of Rockhampton called Maryborough. Its to far south for crocodiles to live but the one from Rockhampton Reptile park may have wandered there. The crocodile they photographed seems to be used to being trapped as it wont get in any of the traps they lay for it. If it was Ashley's crocodile it would be used to fresh water and the climate as well as being used to being trapped as the reptile park would trap them all the time to move them around different enclosures. That wasn't the only time I had my face stabbed and hacked into there was one other time. I was again rendered homeless and was hanging around with a guy called Jeffrey. Jeffrey used to be a millionaire he owned CQ Screens Queensland's largest window screen supplier but he got involved in drugs and spent most of what he had. We were living at the homeless shelter on Alma street and shoplifting when I received a call from Sara saying she wanted to come and see me. I couldn't say no if I did she would come and find me anyway so I told her to meet me at Paddy Go Easy a bar just up the road in central Rockhampton. I had just arrived in the bar when I was greeted by Sara "2 bourbons and coke please" she said. I ordered her a premixed can of bourbon and coke instead as it contained around 2 drinks and was cheaper but Sara insisted on two seven ounce glasses. After getting the drinks Sara suggested we sit out the back as there was no one else out there and I noticed she had died her hair from blonde to black. I sat down at a table and started reading the newspaper when Sara has knocked both her glasses of bourbon off the table. I thought it was just a accident and she appeared to be cleaning it up. She then went into the toilet to pick out a suitable piece of broken glass then came back and jammed into the left side of my ear throat and eye as many times as she could. Sara then ran to the bar screaming to call police saying I had stabbed myself. The police station was only a block away and they came on foot. If it wasn't for Jeffrey being a witness she may have gotten away with it. Glassing is very brutal as it takes hours of scraping the wound clean and removing the glass fragments. By the time they were ready to sow me up I was screaming like a baby sore from them scraping out the glass. I think the general idea Sara had was to say I tried to commit suicide or something to that effect but her whole story became untangled as she told too many lies. She pleaded guilty to unlawful wounding and spent 2 years in prison.

CHAPTER 19

Unsung Heroes

I've been to prison 14 times so I've probably got some story's to tell. Mortimer was a friend of mine, he did our laundry day in and day out. At Capricornia Correctional Centre each block or pod had its own laundry and washing machines. Mortimer had no release date and its one of the saddest reports of a miscarriage of justice I've ever heard. Mortimer prior to being incarcerated had about $800,000 from a compensation payout. He was caught with 2 ecstasy tablets and $10 worth of weed and for that he had been in prison for about 3 years from what he told me without being convicted. Of course it doesn't take a rocket scientist to work out that his money also seemed to get lost in the system. Capricornia Correctional Centre was no stranger to misconduct and corruption. We weren't allowed to read the newspapers or watch the news for a while as there was a corruption inquiry taking place and prison guards and police officers we knew were on trial. I know of people being murdered in the prison involving prison guards, criminals and even police but that's another story. Furthermore about the corruption inquiry police were caught paying criminals serving long sentences to do all sorts of things including pleading guilty to armed robbery's where the money was never recovered. They were told to say they spent it so police could divide it up between themselves. The criminals would be sentenced concurrently meaning serving 2 sentences at once and they would not receive any extra time. Police were also caught paying criminals $1000 at a time straight into there prison bank accounts and that had been going on for decades. Dirty deeds done dirt cheap wasn't just a rock and roll song at Capricornia Correction Centre. Anyway Mortimer rarely complained because any time he did they took him to the nuthouse and experimented on his mind with different psych drugs. I guess after all the torment he had been through he was numb to what had happened and happy to still be alive after knowing the things we all knew. Mortimer had made a new friend as well a known standover man Anderson had been making him cups of tea and acting like his bitch. I could see it coming as Anderson used to beat up someone on average once every 4 weeks. He was paranoid about his crimes and thought he needed to assert some dominance to survive the 6 or 7 years he was serving. Being hardened to the system It stood out to me what Anderson was doing. He was singleing out older opponent's that had a bit of a reputation in there day but now lacked the youth and testosterone to be able to beat him, especially after Anderson deployed his trademark tactics they would have no hope. Friendship is something that is earnt and grows in time its not something that just happens. Anderson Would make a friend of the guy he was going to attack. He would pretend to be the best friend ever by making cups of tea and constantly having there back. This behaviour of Anderson's would usually last about 6 days and by now the victim has no idea of what's about to happen to them and they've fallen into a sense of false security and let there guard down. Anderson would usually hit from behind without warning and throw as many punches into the back of the head as it took or until he was fully spent. I tried to warn Mortimer but what do you say? how can you be sure that that's what's going to happen? and then if Anderson finds out you have said something you'll have to deal with the serial pest yourself. Regardless I said to Mortimer "what the fuck bro your my mate not Andersons he's up to no good" I told him "try to stay away from him" but Mortimer had bought into the friends trick and merely said "narr he's ok he's trying to be nice". When you shut the laundry door you couldn't hear the clanging of the washing machines and dryers. It was almost sound proof. I kept my eye on

Anderson every time he entered the laundry and I actually happened to watch it unfold. Anderson shut the door behind him while Mortimer continued reading the news paper with his head down leaning over it on the bench. Without warning Anderson just pounded into him from behind and he didn't stand a chance. No one could hear Mortimer's screams and its not allowed for anyone to tell the prison guards what's happening as you would then be a dog. Blood was spattered all up the walls and Mortimer was transferred to the hospital where he underwent surgery to fix his dislodged retinas in his eyes. A couple of weeks had passed and everyone forgot about what happened to Mortimer. Anderson had beaten up someone else by then and I was busy writing a book 6 hours a day and when I wasn't writing I was working out. I had a pretty easy stay on that occasion as I had a guy called Fatboy Weeding running a shop for me and he also cooked every meal I ate from off the buy up so I didn't have to eat prison food. I worked out really hard, harder then anyone else in that block or unit and I was doing huge amounts of chin-ups. I would do 13 chin-ups then two sets of 12 chin-ups then 11 chin-ups and two sets of 10 chin-ups and I would work my way down to 1 chin-up and with pushups I did 70 50 30 70 50 30 and repeat that one more time where as most guys only did 4 sets of 10 pushups, my arms were huge. It was now obvious that Anderson saw me as a threat and he was also jealous as he started trying to make friends with me walking laps and talking to me all the time in between my sets. I saw it coming straight away. Just like with Mortimer he pretended to be my friend for about 6 days even making me cups of tea when I already had Fatboy making them for me. Sure as shit sticks to a blanket after about 6 days of him pretending he was my best friend he tried to take a swing into the back of my head but missed as I had glanced over my shoulder at the same time. I turned and grabbed him and pulled him close so my forehead was touching his and all his punches had no choice but to swing around the back of my head not hitting me at all or just brushing into me. Soon as he was worn out from throwing punches I pushed him out then back in and head butted him before throwing him head first into the bottom of the cage and concrete floor. At first I didn't realize that I had actually won the fight

I was just glad it was over as I didn't really want to fight. Walking away into the air-conditioned section of our housing unit one of Andersons mates said "quick go clean yourself up before the screws see it" it was at that moment I realized I wasn't bleeding and hadn't been hurt. Usually when there is a fight the screws (prison guards) grab both of you and lock you in the detention unit for a week. It acts as a deterrent to stop fights happening as a week without proper food exercise tv and grooming facility's is pretty hard to handle but on this occassion they chose not to see it. Over the next few days there was a very uneasy feeling about the place. There was tension and everyone was on edge waiting for another fight between me and Anderson to erupt. About 5days had passed and one my friends had came into the prison but he was placed in another yard. The friend was the former CQ Screens owner and boss J Ross. I really wanted to catch up with him so I sent a message over for him to meet me up the gym in the morning so we could spend about 1 hour together. What happens is there are 4 housing blocks joined together in a X shape separated in the middle by what they call a fish bowl in which the screws sit in to get a panoramic view of everyone. In the mornings 15 men from each of the 4 housing blocks would assemble on the walkway along with about 15 workers and another 20 men going to the education facility's totalling around 95 men. Every morning without fail around 95 men would be out on that walkway. The next morning I rushed to be one of the 15 allowed to go to the gym and I put my name down, grabbed my identification card and exited through the airlock doors onto the walkway. To my surprise there was only one man standing up at one of the gates a guy called Crawford and I immediately knew something wasn't right. All of a sudden I heard the airlock doors opening and closing meaning someone was coming out, it was Anderson and a guy called Mick. Anderson never ever went to the gym work or education and neither did his mate Mick. Warning bells were ringing in my head and I remembered Mick approaching me a few days earlier saying" Demo im involved in something that I don't want to be involved in and I don't know what to do about it" he was really stressing to me that he had no choice in the matter what ever it was. At that moment I realized there was going to be trouble so I just walked back down the walkway towards Anderson and Mick and managed to pass them unscathed. I walked back through the airlock doors into my housing unit and within 60 seconds alarms went off and the entire prison went into lockdown mode. Lockdown mode meant everyone had to get locked in there cells immediately. The entire maximum side of the prison 500 men in 10 housing units lockdown really quick and everyone is secure within about 2 minutes. Screws came straight into my cell asking questions I didn't understand. They were asking about a shiv (home made knife) "where did the shiv come from" they asked and of course I didn't know anything about it. Apparently someone had slipped a note into the screws fish bowl saying there was a shiv in the unit and if they didn't find it quickly Demo which is what they called me would be killed. They asked had there been any trouble in the last few days, any fights they asked but I told them no so they left. They started going cell by cell searching everyone but by the time they had searched 6 cells they had the info they required and grabbed the 3 people responsible and removed them. Pine was 1 he was a serial killer into wija boards like a foreplay before he committed homicides. Pine had already murdered 2 people in prison. I thought Pine and I were pretty close as he opened up to me about the wija board killings that brought him into custody but he was the person who owned the shiv. Anderson and Mick were sent straight to other prisons as well as it turns out Anderson was furious that I beat him in a fight and was going to kill me over it in the gym area as there's a spot off camera. I was disgusted to find out 500 people, a lot of whom are supposed to be my friends knew that I was going to be killed and they knew this for a couple of days in advance and still no one told me. Mortimer finally had his day in court. They called him up and the judge was furious at the police for having him there so long and ordered his immediate release. I remember him coming back through the doors asking me for a address he could go to.

CHAPTER 20

Surrender Sweet Surrender

Because police used to knock the doors in of the houses I rented and the pub rooms I rented I couldn't rent a house anywhere in Rockhampton. I couldn't work because of my criminal record after being in prison 14 times in 7 years. My record had hundreds of charges so no one would employ me. Eventually Centrelink which is Australia's Social Security offered me a pension because of those reasons as I was handicapped by it all. I used to have to go to court most weeks as I was still facing a lot of charges and one time I made several appearances in the 5 day week and in all different jurisdiction of the courts. I was always on the news and sometimes murderers would get upset when there trial would be overlooked by news crews and only footage and news story's about me were shown. I fought and fought as hard as I could and I never ever confessed or plead guilty to anything except the last time I was caught cooking meth. I was in prison and they told me to plead guilty "plead guilty and you can go home today" the lawyer said. After 6 months in prison going home to down graded charges of attempt to cook meth was too good to refuse so I surrendered. I was still going to court and slowly getting warn down by the system and now I was completely homeless. When I say homeless I mean sleeping in parks with a broken bottle in my hand for protection. I slept at night which was something a lot of homeless people don't do as its not safe to sleep in parks by yourself at night. Most homeless would sleep during the day and by night they would sit in a all-night cafe or places like that. I was trapped in Rockhampton still going to court for the remaining charges that were pending and the homeless shelter would no longer let me stay there. Its funny when I was selling drugs and had plenty of money they welcomed me with open arms all the time but now I really needed them they just assumed I could fend for myself and would turn me away. The only way I could get a roof over my head was if I drank a bottle of wine and pretended I was drunk so the drunk tank would take me in. The drunk tank in Rockhampton was a place police took drunken aboriginals too so they could sober up and have a shower and a feed. To some homeless aboriginals it was the only thing that kept them alive as it was the only time they ate. The rest of the time they would consume the cheapest available alcohol sometimes drinking mentholated spirits. When I started drinking it was just to get the drunk tank to allow me to stay there over night. I had been sober and off the drink for about 7 years. I would buy a bottle of bowlers run for 3 dollar's and take a couple of sips of the low grade stuff and pour some on my clothing to pretend I was drunk. It gets really really hot during the day in Rockhampton so I would do this about 4 o'clock in the afternoon. It felt great to get into the air-conditioning and have a shower. They would give you clean pyjamas to put on and let you go to bed in the cool where it was safe to dream of better things. It wasn't long before I was actually tolerating the taste of the cheap wine and drinking it to numb myself. It took away the anguish and seemed to cushion or smother the shame of how low I had sunk. I worked out I had no real friends in Rockhampton as its true there is no honour among thieves and everyone I knew was either from prison or a customer of mine or someone wanting to use me to unload drugs. To my surprise my brother actually talked to my parents whom I hadn't really seen for over 12 years. He told them I was sleeping in parks and had become just like the old guy you see sleeping on a park bench or begging for money. My brother tracked me down and convinced me to ring my parents who said they wanted me to come home. When I first returned they made me sleep in a little room outside by the laundry so they could lock me out of the house at night as they were scared of me. I was still facing charges in Rockhampton so I had no choice but to return there to go to court. While travelling the 2000 kilometres up the east coast by train I would stop over with homeless mates in Brisbane and sleep by the river bank. Brisbane was half way and I had bumped into a guy called Justin in Brisbane when I was on the way down the first time. Justin spent years homeless in Rockhampton and he showed me where to get free food. He also took me to where he would sleep in a group so it was safer. They slept underneath a over pass roadway almost like a bridge right on the Brisbane river. I must have made a dozen trips up and down and I stopped to see Justin every time. Eventually my parents said if I could give up smoking and the drugs they would let me stay inside the house at night. My parents had a beautiful home so it was hard to resist. I went to see a drug and alcohol service who put me on a suboxone program like methadone. The trouble with that was I had to attend every day for 3 months before they could dose me from a chemist. The clinic was 200 kilometres away from my parents place so they rented me a motel room just up the road from the clinic. At the motel I met a guy named Nathan and during the course of conversation I mentioned that I had just finished going to court and naturally he asked what for. When I told him it was for cooking meth he was very interested and offered to pay for everything if I showed him how to do it. I had no money at the time and the opportunity to make $6000 worth of meth at his expense lured me in and before I knew it I was back in prison at Kempsey Correctional Centre. Nathan in the course of rounding up the materials needed to cook with had told the wrong people and police actually brought him home. Everything was in his room and it wasn't until 2 days after his arrest that they arrested me. It was on the news for 3 days running and eventually he told them it was me. Mum and Dad came to visit every weekend even though it was about a 4 hour drive to get to the prison. Prison's in the state of N.S.W were different to Queensland as Queensland jails are all single cells where as N.S.W has shared cells and you can end up sharing with anyone. The one thing I hated about jail is you cant choose your company. It doesn't seem to matter where you go in life there will always be someone you don't like and someone who doesn't like you. When I was released I was completely drug and alcohol free and had almost given up smoking so my parents allowed me to sleep inside the house. To me after 14 years on the road and in prisons it was luxury. Now that I wasn't smoking, drinking and taking drugs I started to save money. It wasn't a huge amount of money but it was more then I had ever saved in my life. Prior to that I had always spent every dollar I had the more I had the more I spent. I got talking on Facebook with a guy in Indonesia called Bams. Bams said I should look on a site called A Date In Asia for a wife. He said a Asian wife would make a much better wife for me then a Australian so I looked at the site. There were thousands of beautiful young woman to choose from so many that I simply couldn't choose. I thought being that good-looking they must have other men writing to them and therefore I would have to compete. I scrolled and scrolled and eventually I came across this girl with a ugly giant mole right between her eyes. I immediately felt for the girl but I didn't feel lust I felt sorrow. I thought what a poor girl no one will choose her so I wrote to her. If it wasn't for the ugly mole she would be quite attractive. I wrote asking that if I sent the money to have the mole removed would she choose to remove it. She immediately responded and relayed how much that mole embarrassed her. Her name was Jolibee she was very poor and from the Philippines. I knew if I sent the money it would likely be spent on food but I told her it was for the mole to be removed. I've never transferred money overseas before so I went to see my bank who told me it was a simple straight forward transfer and all I needed was a Philippines bank account. Jolibee didn't have a bank account but they found one for the money to go into. When I went to transfer the money the bank did it easily but then contacted me telling me to come pick up my money as I had been scammed and they somehow pulled the money back from the Philippines account. Jolibee was so upset she wrote and wrote to me via Facebook she was desperate for the money. I thought how could me wanting to give someone money be a scam and I asked Jolibee was there another way and we came up with western union money transfer. Once she had the money she did exactly as I asked and had the mole removed. The transformation was great and the surgeon did a remarkable job hardly leaving a scar. Jolibee and I wrote to each other almost everyday and this continued for about 5 years. She struggled to find food every day sometimes eating only bananas for weeks. The main diet in the Philippines is rice and for jolibee that meant rice by itself but on occasions she flavoured the rice with coffee. I sent money to help when I could but not much just small amounts. I also bought the father a small truck but he purchased one that needed repair assuming I would pay to fix it. Of course I didn't have anymore money and the truck was useless. Jolibee washed clothes by hand in a plastic bucket for her job and she had heaps of customers. She told me it rains all the time there and she could not dry the clothes. It was obvious to me she needed a washing machine and a clothes dryer but I came up with a idea to put clothes lines and washing machines in a shop with blower fans to dry the clothes. I was very happy as Jolibee ended up with 3 shops. The truck I have had fully overhauled and fitted with tyres and other parts so Jolibee could sell it to facilitate the sale of the shops at least that is what she told me. Purchasing everything for the shops was just a scam of Jolibee's this took months to set up 3 shops but in the end It was just make believe and I was merely sending money for her to spend. Most of the characters are now dead. John died of lung cancer and his brother Noel died of a heroin overdose. The other brother Dale died of a heart attack. Ivan Milat is Dead he died in prison from cancer and Roger Rogerson died in prison as well. Debbie, Nicky and Damien are dead along with Sarah Ed and Max and my brother and probably a few others.

May they rest in peace

Tony Bent is serving another life sentence after he shot a bloke in Newcastle. He had just been released after serving ten years for armed robbery from when I knew him and I saw this on Australia's most wanted whilst I was in prison in 2013. Ibrah now has 17 night clubs and wrote a book after he was featured in the underbelly series the golden mile. He was upset that underbelly didn't tell the truth. About the fighting it was always self defence. I found out at a early age if you start a fight without reason you generally lose so I would wait until someone either made me very angry or forced me to fight. At the time I was throwing thousands of punches a day. I did it to keep myself safe as I hitchhiked hundreds of kilometres in and out of the Bowen basin travelling to work.

The End

www.ingramcontent.com/pod-product-compliance
Lightning Source LLC
Chambersburg PA
CBHW020502030426
42337CB00011B/199